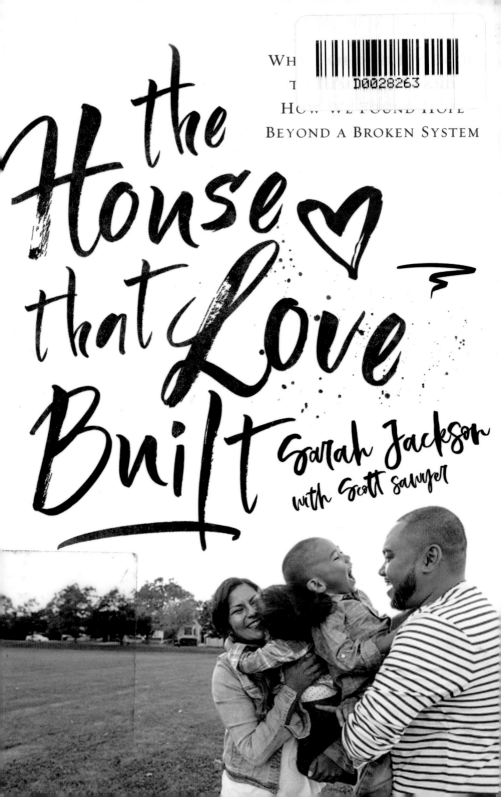

WH...

T...

HOW WE FOUND HOPE

BEYOND A BROKEN SYSTEM

the House ♡ that Love Built

Sarah Jackson

with Scott Sawyer

Sarah Jackson reminds us that one of the holiest things we can do is welcome the stranger. In fact, Jesus says that when we welcome the stranger, we welcome him. And Paul writes in Hebrews that when we show hospitality to foreigners, we may very well be "entertaining angels." But there is a war between faith and fear happening inside each of us. In this dazzling gem of a book, Sarah Jackson dares us to love as big as God loves. She is convinced that the Bible is correct when it says that "love casts out fear." Sarah has chosen love. And she will inspire you to do the same.

—SHANE CLAIBORNE, author; activist; cofounder, Red Letter Christians

Our community's diversity is our strength, a value that I've seen Sarah Jackson lift up every day in her work at Casa de Paz. Casa de Paz has provided a safe harbor for hundreds of people cast aside by our nation's broken immigration system. The story of Casa de Paz is a story of leadership, empathy, and our shared humanity. It's a story about how we have shared obligations toward one another and how we are all better off when we take care of those who need help. As we work to build a more inclusive community, Casa de Paz reminds us what we can achieve when we come together.

—CONGRESSMAN JASON CROW

I have met scores of restless young adults, and my first impression of Sarah was that she was probably just a salsa-dancing idealist. Sarah proved me wrong. She is an incarnational visionary, and this book bears witness to the mustard-seed power of gospel hospitality. Oh, Sarah's still a salsa-dancing idealist. She's just so much more.

—ANTON FLORES-MAISONET, lead founder,
El Refugio and Casa Alterna

Fair warning: you will be changed as you read these pages, because the words themselves are fueled by the unstoppable and upending love of the one who is for, with, and in each and every person on the planet! This story shouts from the rooftops the invitation to follow in the steps of Jesus, with hands reaching and eyes glistening with extravagant and tangible love for all. This book has been crafted *for such a time as this!*

—SARAH DAVISON-TRACY, author; speaker; founder, Seeds of Exchange

Most Americans probably do not realize that our country has an immigrant detention system. They certainly don't know the millions of individuals whom it has entangled in recent years. Sarah Jackson has welcomed thousands of these asylum seekers and other immigrants into her home. This book is the compelling, faith-stretching story of how Sarah founded Casa de Paz and of the remarkable people—both immigrants and native-born Americans—whom God has brought into her life along the way. It's also an urgent wakeup call for the American church to heed Jesus' call to practice hospitality.

—MATTHEW SOERENS, US Director of Church
Mobilization and Advocacy, World Relief

This book reminds us that immigration is about immigrants and that immigrants are people deeply loved by God. Sarah Jackson demonstrates with her life how we, as followers of Christ, stand with all people wherever they may be—from the womb to the tomb, from the belly to the border!

—ROBERT GELINAS, lead pastor, Colorado Community Church

My visit to Casa de Paz taught me how to translate American values into concrete actions. I am impressed by Sarah's passion for and dedication to welcoming immigrants with unconditional, nonjudgmental love and care. This book shows perfect examples of how welcoming the stranger is meant to be.

—BASEL MOUSSLLY, Program Manager for Migrant Services,
Lutheran Immigration and Refugee Service

I have known Sarah since she started Casa de Paz in her apartment several years ago. I am recommending this book because her story of helping immigrants is unique and fascinating and everyone needs to know it.

—JUAN CARLOS GUTIERREZ, News Director, Univision Colorado

With passion and candor, Sarah Jackson takes us on her faith-based journey to open the doors of Casa de Paz, a Denver-area nonprofit that provides shelter and support to immigrants recently released from detention. The journey Jackson shares is about the true meaning of hospitality—treating our immigrant neighbors with dignity and respect, and seeing in their experiences family ties that should be strengthened and fostered, not broken. This book is a call to action that highlights the heartwrenching, beautiful stories of the immigrants that Sarah and Casa volunteers assist and learn from, and how daily acts of kindness can change the world. The best of humanity is found in these pages.

—ELIZABETH R. ESCOBEDO, Associate Professor
of History, University of Denver

The commandment to love our neighbor is easier said than done. Sarah and Casa de Paz can say it's easy to do because they are doing it and showing all of us that it is possible to be hospitable and loving and caring. Love knows no borders.

—AMILCAR VALENCIA, cofounder, Executive
Director, El Refugio Ministry

I've known Sarah for a while and one of the things that hits me is her passion for immigration and pragmatism. In this book you will get to know someone who responded to a call and went through a process of transformation. This call is not something to be taken lightly, and it's also for a few. We can educate and advocate for a compassionate approach to the complex subject of immigration, but what will make a real difference in the world is having people like Sarah as a witness of compassion and care for the stranger. Thanks, Sarah, for your witness and commitment!

—MAURICIO C, Minister for Church Planting,
Mennonite Mission Network

Against so many odds, Sarah Jackson has built not only a house of peace but also a powerful movement of healing and hope. This movement is about not only restoring immigrants' dignity where it has been lost but also helping people break through misconceptions and damaging narratives and move toward living out our greatest call: love God, love others. I have known Sarah since she started Casa de Paz and have watched the inspiration she's catalyzed across different groups of people in deep and transforming ways. Her book will inspire, challenge, and stir hearts into action, which is exactly what the world needs right now more than ever.

—Kathy Escobar, co-pastor, The Refuge; author,
Practicing: Changing Yourself to Change the World

Sarah Jackson's commitment to welcoming and caring for immigrants is not based on platitudes but is lived out in daily care and concern for immigrants' welfare. At a time when the vitriol around immigrants and immigration—rooted in deep partisan divides—is at an all-time high, Jackson's story crafts a new narrative that can lead us to live out the call of Christ to love our neighbors and welcome strangers. We need new voices, new leadership, and a new way forward to be the people of God, ready and willing to deeply engage a hurting world. Sarah Jackson is that new leader.

—Michelle Ferrigno Warren, activist; author, *The Power of Proximity*

the House that Love Built

the House that Love Built

Why I Opened My Door to Immigrants and How We Found Hope beyond a Broken System

Sarah Jackson

with Scott Sawyer

ZONDERVAN BOOKS

ZONDERVAN BOOKS

The House That Love Built
Copyright © 2020 by Sarah Jackson

Requests for information should be addressed to:
Zondervan, *3900 Sparks Dr. SE, Grand Rapids, Michigan 49546*

Zondervan titles may be purchased in bulk for educational, business, fundraising, or sales promotional use. For information, please email SpecialMarkets@Zondervan.com.

ISBN 978-0-310-35562-5 (softcover)
ISBN 978-0-310-35566-3 (audio)
ISBN 978-0-310-35565-6 (ebook)

Published in association with the literary agency of WordServe Literary Group, Ltd, www.wordserveliterary.com.

This is a work of nonfiction. Some names and other identifying characteristics have been changed to protect the privacy of the individuals involved.

Cover design: Studio Gearbox
Cover photo: kate_sept2004 | Getty Images
Interior design: Denise Froehlich

Printed in the United States of America

20 21 22 23 24 / LSC / 10 9 8 7 6 5 4 3 2 1

This story is dedicated to my family,
those I have known since birth,
and also to my family of strangers, those I've met, have
yet to meet, and may not meet: my angels unaware.

Contents

All persons depicted in this book are real. There are no composites. Some names and identifying details have been changed for their protection.

Acknowledgments

Thank you to every migrant who has crossed our threshold, lives that write a continuous, beautiful story, as they have for thousands of years. To all who covered Casa de Paz in prayers before it existed, and those of every faith who pray for us today. To every friend of Casa de Paz, stranger, advocate, and official who contributed to this book, mentioned or not. To Zondervan and WordServe for steady faith, especially Stephanie Smith, Keely Boeving, and Brian Phipps, and for skill and vision from Greg Johnson, Alyssa Karhan, Alicia Kasen, Amanda Halash, David Morris, and particularly John Sloan, storytelling master over decades. To Anasi Russo Garrido and Nadine Jackson for invaluable critical feedback. To Scott Sawyer for faith in our mustard seed of a story and for standing alongside the Casa as we grow up together, for not only telling our story but being part of it—for holding the arm of the elderly grandmother released from detention as she took her first steps of freedom, for sitting with me in court as we shed tears of thanksgiving over our friend receiving his God-given freedom, for mourning with family members as they realized they may never see their loved one again; your words tell a story of hope, a gift to us all. And to the Casa community: I like to think Jesus has this book on his handcrafted wooden coffee table, and each time he reads it, his eyes light up and he says, "Well done, good and faithful servants." You all heed a great call: "The plain fact is that the planet does not need more successful people. But it does desperately need more peacemakers, healers, restorers, storytellers, and lovers of every kind" (David W. Orr, *Ecological Literacy*).

Introduction

ONE COKE, TWO STRAWS

For a tomboy kindergartner, it doesn't get any better than date night with your dad. Your cool older brother and cute baby sister are nowhere in sight. So maybe your shoes don't go with your outfit and maybe your hair didn't get brushed the way your mom wanted, though she did her best while you fidgeted to get moving. Now sitting across from your smiling, work-weary dad, you scatter crust crumbs all over the table at his favorite pizza joint because that's the kind of exciting night it is. It doesn't matter that you each get only one slice of pepperoni because the family budget is tight ever since your talented mom homeschooled you instead of working for pay, or that you and your dad have to split one coke with two straws. For one night a month, you have him all to yourself, and all day long you'd smacked your lips at the thought of that bubbly, syrupy, ice-cold coke together. It's a feeling like no other in the world.

Fast-forward about twenty years: I shared a meal with another dad, one about my age. And he reminded me of my own.

I met him in a migrant shelter in Mexico, just across the international border from Arizona, while on a church trip. The shelter was for men recently deported from the US. The dad I met looked, sounded, and spoke like a US citizen. That's because he grew up in the US. And he'd grown up thinking he was a citizen. As an infant, Agustín had been brought to the United States by his parents, never knowing that none of his family was documented. When he was ready to get his driver's license, excited as any teen would be, his parents sat him down and told him.

The news turned Agustín's world upside down. He didn't know what to do or think. He churned inside with a mixture of betrayal and a sudden fear for his family. He didn't know how to think about the future or whether he even had one.

In the end, Agustín did what so many undocumented young people do: He went on with life as he'd known it. He married his sweetheart, a US citizen. He started a business and hired people. He was active in his church. He and his wife had two sons and now a daughter soon would be born. But at age thirty, as he drove to pick up his boys from elementary school, he was stopped by a policeman. He was driving *under* the speed limit in a school zone.

Agustín was arrested and handcuffed. And he was deported.

The dad sitting across from me eating soup in a migrant shelter was forcibly removed from the only world he knew. He had to give up his business and say goodbye to the most precious things in his life—his two sons and his then-pregnant wife. All for lack of a piece of paper.

I couldn't—or, rather, didn't—want to believe what I was hearing. My country wouldn't do this to someone like the guy sitting across from me. I thought everybody who married someone from the US was automatically a citizen. That's how it used to be, anyway.

I was convinced the guy must have done something really wrong. The words I'd heard to describe him were *illegal* and *alien*. I believed like a lot of people: we need to make our borders harder to get through.

But Agustín didn't look or talk like a dangerous or sneaky

person. He talked about his wife and sons the same way all of my friends did. When it came to his ten-month-old daughter, his voice strained: He just wanted to hold her, he said. He'd never even seen her. She had been born after he was deported.

I searched his eyes.

My own daughter date nights with my father told me everything about my worth in the world. How were Agustín's children able to know that kind of worth if they couldn't look into his eyes? How could he be torn apart from them this way?

That one moment, at a shelter full of deported men in Mexico, changed everything for me. It led me to reexamine my focus as a Christian.

"'Love the LORD your God with all your heart, all your soul, and all your mind.' This is the first and greatest commandment. A second is *equally important*: 'Love your neighbor as yourself.' The entire law and all the demands of the prophets are based on *these two commandments*" (Matt. 22:37–40 NLT, my emphases). God makes it simple for us: Want to fulfill the law? Put yourself in the shoes of someone in front of you. Do for them what you would want somebody to do for you.

I'd never been in the shoes of someone like Agustín—not even close to it. I couldn't change his situation. But I did know I could do *something*.

And so, at age twenty-four, I decided to walk alongside people like Agustín and his family, people whose lives are devastated, sometimes torn apart permanently, by our immigration system.

In Denver, where I live, there's a massive federal immigrant detention facility. More than a thousand people are held there at any given time—people like Agustín—while their case is being decided. Until recently, nobody on the Front Range of Colorado seemed to know the facility is there. That's the case in most cities. And most people held inside never see anyone they know. Many of them are held there for years.

I realized I could come alongside these neighbors of mine in a very simple way: I could visit them. If their families lived a great distance away, I could invite them into my home so they could visit their detained loved ones without having to pay for hotels. By merely opening my door, I could reconnect families who were separated from each other.

I soon found out that people detained in the facility were being released nearly every day and many had nowhere to go. They were from other countries with no relatives in the US, and they weren't legally allowed to work, so they were left vulnerable, helpless to feed themselves or get shelter.

Last year, in 2018, 70 million people around the world were displaced—one out of every hundred human beings on the earth. The vast majority migrate in desperation, fleeing war, persecution, disease, violence, government oppression, starvation. In the US, about 400,000 people are held in immigrant detention each year. No one should be jailed for seeking safety or security, especially those with children. Most people don't want to abandon their culture—the scents, the songs, the familiar soil. And nobody wants to leave their loved ones behind.

Their plight led me to open the door of my cramped, six-hundred-square-foot apartment to host those released people. I decided to name my home Casa de Paz—"House of Peace." That's what I wanted them to experience as they navigated the traumatic journey of immigration.

From the outset, I saw faces that reminded me of my own family. Alicia, a white mom, drove in from Nebraska with her four kids to visit their dad, who was detained in Denver. A West African, he'd been jailed for more than a year for being undocumented. He had lived and worked in the US for years, and his wife and children were American citizens. But now the whole family was nervous because he could be deported at any time and not be allowed back for ten years, if ever.

As I stirred a pot of soup for them, Alicia laid out their dilemma. With her husband gone, she and the kids had been evicted. Alicia moved them into an abandoned house on the outskirts of town. It had no electricity or running water.

After dinner, as the kids headed to bed, Alicia told me this was the first hot meal they'd had in a long time. With no way to heat food, they'd been eating meals out of cans. She thanked me and hugged me tightly, not knowing she squeezed a tear from my eye. Her hug felt exactly like one my mother would give. Suddenly, I realized what a simple, hot bowl of soup might mean: that someone cares about your family.

Simple things. But they're luxuries to a newly single parent panicked by what the future may hold for her family. Alicia's story was not unique.

To see kids traumatized because they can't touch their father through thick plexiglass in a detention center, to hear them say a tearful goodbye because he might be deported, to talk to a detained mom separated from her child at the border with no idea where that child is being held in the US immigration system—it's almost too much to bear.

And yet they are why, in eight years, I've welcomed nearly three thousand guests into my home—people from seventy-three countries and from across the US. Some are families like Alicia's who come to visit, and some are people newly released from detention. Casa de Paz is no longer a tiny, cramped apartment but an actual house—a nice one, on an average block, in an average neighborhood. It may look a lot like yours. Three bedrooms, two baths, a basement with room for guests, and a

nice big tree out front. Like any house on our block, it all centers
on family. Joyful meals and tearful reunions.

In that short time, more than two thousand people have volunteered at Casa de Paz to carry off enormously important jobs:
picking up bewildered people released from detention, cooking
meals for them, accompanying them to their court dates, helping
to arrange their travel to reunite with loved ones. And we visit
with those inside detention, every day of the week, having made
more than a thousand visits last year alone. On Sundays, fifty or
more volunteers visit in shifts. At Christmas and on Valentine's
Day we write holiday cards and include a candy bar for everyone
in detention, so they don't feel forgotten. We do anything we
can think of to alleviate their pain, to make them feel worthy of
lovingkindness—because God says they are. Nobody gets paid
for doing this; everyone's a volunteer. That includes me. We all
want to be part of Casa de Paz. Together we've heard thousands
of immigrant stories, and not one has been easy to hear. But we
all keep coming because of something intangible.

I know exactly what it is.

If you don't think love actually makes a difference in the
world, we have a story to tell you.

This love story has caught the attention of decision-makers
around the world. The United Nations sent a representative to
study Casa de Paz as a model for immigrant support programs
around the world. A congressman gathers us at his quarterly
immigration table. A congresswoman involves us in a monthly
phone-in conference. A senator and his staff consult with us.
Candidates from both sides of the aisle visit, and one left in tears.
One congressman spent an afternoon volunteering at Casa de
Paz. College professors send their students to intern with us.
Elementary-school teachers bring their classes to volunteer. A
historic denomination asked us to join them as a congregation

because they say we're fulfilling the mission of the church: "for whoever loves others has fulfilled the law" (Rom. 13:8).

I hear a lot about the law from people. Many fellow Christians focus solely on one aspect of immigration: lawbreaking. I've stopped counting the times someone has threatened, "I'm calling ICE [US Immigration and Customs Enforcement] to come shut you down and arrest all the illegals you harbor." I have to tell them that ICE is one of our biggest sources for the guests we host. We often get calls from guards at the detention center when an immigrant is about to be released. Still, the objection I hear most is, "Immigrants should come here the right way." They don't realize that the people showing up at our borders seeking asylum from danger *have* arrived the right way. Anyone claiming asylum has to be *in our country* to do so—that's the law.

Yet I have received death threats for what I do. I'm not sure why it has come to this. I never got a death threat when I made meals for people experiencing homelessness or when I put together hygiene packs for at-risk youth. So why for a group that's equally, if not more, at risk?

I was given an amazing childhood by loving, sacrificing Christian parents. I was exposed to all kinds of church experiences, in a range of denominations. My siblings and I learned to serve sick people, we helped build houses for families in Mexico, we demonstrated for biblical causes. When I left home, I got a job on staff with a thriving megachurch and organized service trips to Africa. I helped start a homeless ministry. I took a position with an international children's outreach. Today, I have a great job with a Christian-based software company that serves churches.

And yet over time, my head somehow got filled with negative thoughts about immigrants. How? Maybe because I never knew one. (Or thought I didn't.) Or maybe because I didn't hear sermons on how God views displaced people from other countries.

From the very beginning, Christians took in migrants, a legacy rooted in Judaism, which gave foreigners equal standing in significant ways. The apostle Paul urged his readers to keep up hospitality, a word that literally means "love for the stranger" (*philo* = love, *xenia* = stranger). Hosting foreigners and strangers was an everyday, core practice for Christians over nearly two millennia. It was a calling for everyone. And they made strangers feel like family because God said they *were* family.

After I served dinner to a young African man just released from detention, he said softly, "It feels like home here." He had no idea how deeply those words went into me. To know we belong, to know we matter, to know our worth in the world, even from a stranger—isn't that what we all want? Isn't that what's behind Christ's two-part Great Commandment to love God and our neighbor?

When we create that kind of space—one where displaced, traumatized people feel they're home, even for a few hours—together we experience a bit of heaven on earth. I believe that every small act of hospitality is a step toward Jesus' desire: "Your kingdom come, your will be done, *on earth as it is in heaven*" (Matt. 6:10, my emphasis). When someone is treated the way God values them, we all touch heaven. "Lord, when did we see you hungry and feed you, or thirsty and give you something to drink? When did we see you a stranger and invite you in . . . ?' The King will reply, 'Truly I tell you, whatever you did for one of the least of these brothers and sisters of mine, you did for me'" (Matt. 25:37–38, 40).

A world of transformation can start with a pot of soup in a tiny apartment. It did with mine.

PART 1

Eyes To See

If we have no peace, it is because we have forgotten that we belong to each other.

—MOTHER TERESA

The story of Casa de Paz is about two stories coming together.

—RENÉ GALINDO, PROFESSOR OF EDUCATION,
UNIVERSITY OF COLORADO DENVER

CHAPTER 1

We Were Strangers Taken In

*To look life straight in the eye, to see its pain and
to see its beauty—this is an essential part of
glimpsing the way forward.*

—RICHARD ROHR, "KNOWLEDGE OF GOOD AND EVIL"

"We invite you . . ."

I've always loved those words. They carry the power to change the world. Yet when I read them on my screen one frosty December morning in 2010, change was the last thing on my mind. I absolutely loved everything about my life.

The email had come to my boss, the senior pastor at Vanguard Church in Colorado Springs. Sorting through the avalanche of emails that appeared in his inbox was the boring part of my job as the church's assistant administrator. I thrived at the rest— organizing conferences, phone meetings, travel arrangements, overseas trips—and loved the challenge of doing it all for *two* bosses, him and the executive pastor. My mom said I had a highly developed logistical gift like my dad's—he's a chip-test engineer—so that when I shot out church emails full of info or instructions to large groups, people felt compelled to write back to "Mrs. Jackson." Most didn't know they were addressing some-one barely in her twenties.

It made me grateful for all those daily lists Mom handed us as homeschoolers. Endless chores and tasks, homework, lists, and *lists* of lists—it seemed like a lot to little kids. But when you grow up with a mom who makes fast friends with strangers in the grocery line, the people part becomes easy too. Whenever my mother heard a foreign lilt, she sought out the speaker, implor-ing, "Your accent is so beautiful. May I ask where you're from?"

At the end of my workday, after I checked off my last box, I'd head to my job as coach of the JV girls volleyball team at St. Mary's, where my sister Anna was fielding scholarship offers. My roommate, Becca, had the same kind of energy I did, and we lived as two entry-level working girls feeling rich in every possible way. Colorado Springs in 2010 was still a small town to some, but for Christian women in their twenties who had a big enough dating pool to narrow down their lists for the perfect guy, life felt, well, perfect.

The only thing I could have used more of was travel. I'd been to Swaziland (now Eswatini), Africa, with the church on a short-term mission—a trip I organized, of course. So on a blue-white winter morning, one unassuming email invitation got me thinking. I was just about to delete the message when two words on the screen jumped out: "trip" and "free."

It was from Catholic Charities. I hadn't heard of them. "An educational trip to learn about border issues."

Hmm. Would the senior pastor consider it? I checked his calendar for February. A good time for a trip to Mexico. Pina coladas on the beach. Then I read, "To learn what the Bible has to say about immigration. . . . join a contingent of pastors from your area."

Our senior pastor was booked that weekend. So was the executive pastor.

"All expenses paid."

Whoa—all expenses? Perhaps a responsible church staffer could go in the pastors' place. And hide her tan lines when she returned.

I formulated a plan. I'd petition for the time off, craft my reply, and request permission to represent our pastoral staff, who were "regrettably unavailable." Our church community would greatly benefit from the gracious offer. Or so I told the pastors and Catholic Charities.

Turns out Tucson can get really cold in February. I didn't know this. Forty degrees! The hotel's outdoor pool was closed. And I didn't notice any beaches and wasn't offered any pina coladas on the shuttle ride from the airport.

Gathered in the hotel lobby when I arrived were seven ministers, five women and two men. Were all these women really pastors? I'd only vaguely heard of their churches, though they were all in the Springs. I approached two women who were laughing so hard I took them for long-lost friends. It turned out they'd just met. Deb Walker was from the big Methodist church downtown, and Clare Twomey pastored the United Church of Christ. I'd never known a woman pastor, and now I was at a convention of them.

No one in the group knew each other. And nobody had much of an idea what to expect of the next three days. Except Clare. She'd been on a border trip like this before, so we coaxed some of the experience out of her. She was generous—a natural teacher and preacher—and she reeled out facts and stories. Once she got going, her gentle spark flamed into passion. We were going to see some hard things, Clare cautioned, but she referenced a few Bible passages about the treatment of foreigners, and others joined in. I thought I knew the Bible pretty well, having been raised on a steady diet of it. But maybe I wasn't listening when these passages were taught. They weren't familiar.

"It's not a crime, per se, for migrants to come here, by the way," Clare noted.

That was news to me. Weren't they "illegal aliens"? Nobody should get away with breaking the law.

"It's actually not even a misdemeanor," Clare said. "It's an administrative matter having to do with paperwork."

I had no framework to get my head around that. I realized I knew nothing about immigration—zero. I'd been thrown into the deep end of the pool. But that's what the trip was about, after all.

When we crossed the Arizona border into Mexico, I saw why Clare could only hint at it. Entering Agua Prieta, a long, bumpy, potholed road stretched ahead of us. Casting a massive shadow over that crude, dusty road was a series of vast, forty-foot-long electronic billboards. They advertised life in America in gigantic terms. All the products you could buy, the many things you could have—paradise, just out of reach.

Between these billboards stood small stores and vendor shacks. And just above them, in digital glory, were forty-foot images of smiling models. Beyond the commercial area, in a neighborhood where we walked, were dilapidated homes with dirt yards. In the streets, packs of dogs roamed everywhere.

There was a strange energy to the place. We saw a man using a tool to drill a hole in the metal border wall. He was frantic, moving with urgency, until finally Border Patrol officers arrived and caught him. We passed by a yard with about fifty roosters. Someone guessed they were being raised for cockfighting.

What was this world? And to think I could have driven here in a day's time from my gated community in Colorado Springs.

On the morning we went to work in the desert, they appeared like specters on the horizon. Walking toward us, apparitions under a gray canopy of desert cold. About a half dozen of them, bobbing left and right, the weave of weary people on tired legs.

When we saw them, all we could think was how cold they must be. Deb wore her Colorado down jacket, and she was shivering.

We set down the fifty-five-gallon water tank we'd brought to replace the empty one as part of our immersion experience. There were a lot of other tanks like this one placed strategically along known migrant trails. All were donated and maintained by nonprofit groups.

As the travelers drew closer, my heart raced. These were the ones—the people we'd been learning and talking about. I felt—well, starstruck. Here they were in real life!

Yet we were shocked at how young they were. Most looked like teenagers. All were underdressed for the cold. They had one blanket among them, a thin, shabby one. A young woman held it, folded up in her arms. She was pregnant. How was she not shivering? She seemed oblivious to the cold, standing strong against it.

One traveler looked like a typical kid I grew up with. Goatee, sunglasses, and tats, wearing a T-shirt.

"Yo!" he yelled to us. No Spanish accent. He sounded like a US teenager. He gave a familiar little wave, the way one compatriot greets another.

Mark Stephen Adams, our guide, stepped forward to greet them. "Buenos dias."

"Hey, bro," the dude said, extending a hand.

Deb couldn't help grinning. "Dude," she said, "what's your story?"

"Goin' home!"

"Where's that?"

"Ohio, man. To my lady and my little girl. Two years old."

"You're from the US?"

"Grew up there. Since I was little bitty," he said. "Columbus, Ohio! That's my country, man."

He had been deported. But why?

Mark scanned the group. He asked in his soft Carolina inflection, "Do you know where you are?"

"We're headed for Phoenix."

Mark nodded gently. "Has anyone told you how far that is?"

As we would learn, most migrants never know where they are or how far they have to go.

These young people didn't know that once they crossed the border, they were still a three-hour drive from Phoenix. And they were on foot.

Mark told them this in Spanish. I could tell it wasn't easy for him. When their group heard it, some looked confused. Still, none looked fazed.

Mark gave them directions to a place called the Migrant Resource Center, in Agua Prieta. They were very near the border now, he said. Before they tried crossing, they could get food at the center and warm clothes for the rest of their journey.

"Thanks, bro," Ohio dude said.

They walked on.

"Why are they lied to?" Deb asked. "Who would mislead them about the distance they have to go?"

Mark shook his head. There was a reason, he explained—a deception maybe less cruel than it seemed. Their "coyotes"—the paid guides who led them for most of the journey—told them a shorter distance because it would sound doable. If they told them the real distance, the walkers' mental state would have been low from the start. They never would have made it.

I barely slept. I kept picturing the pregnant woman, probably still a teenager.

"Did you see that crappy little beach blanket?" Deb said at

breakfast. She gazed downward, as if she hated what she was about to say. "I hope they get stopped," she said. "They're not going to make it."

The previous day had made me quiet. I was so disoriented. All I could think was, *What is happening?*

Our leader, Mark, must have known what we needed. On the Mexican side of the border, he took us to the home of a pastor friend for dinner. It was a small place made of concrete blocks. One room with a dirt floor, but glowing with warmth. At the center of the room was a picnic-style table, where we all sat. The pastor and his wife moved with a quiet peace, serving us dinner as we sat alongside their three young children.

We were humbled into silence. The warm flour tortillas were delicious. I ate at least a dozen, and the pastor's wife kept serving me more. Her husband spoke in broken English, and Mark translated the rest for us. Clare had a few soft exchanges with the pastor in Spanish. A few others chimed in with questions, but we felt awkward. The inner barriers erected by our first-world thinking made us self-conscious.

For Mark and the pastor, though, it was as if this were any other day in their lives. They didn't act like two people in ministry together. They acted the way lifelong friends do.

Someone asked the pastor, "Do you know anyone who has died in the desert?"

He nodded calmly. His wife nodded too. And so we heard stories.

It began to sink in with me how different others' lives were. So different from the life I knew.

And it dawned on me: We weren't there to help this pastor's family. We weren't there to build something for them. No one expected them to be grateful that we came to their home. We were there for one thing: fellowship. To share joys and sorrows, humor and hopes, the way friends and family do: on equal ground. It was humbling.

Back in the hotel lounge, Clare pondered it. "That," my new friend pointed out, tapping the arm of her chair, "was hospitality."

Hospitality. Was that what we just had?

"We're strangers," Clare said. "He invited us in. And he treated us like family. You felt that, didn't you?"

I did. But I'd thought hospitality was something else. Like, throwing a party and being a good host. What we experienced in the pastor's home was different. That's what Clare was getting at. This family wasn't self-conscious or afraid to open up to us.

So why were we? Why was it so awkward for us?

When you're in the desert, it's easier to picture the biblical stories you know. The next day on our desert picnic, we reflected on some of the Bible's well-known passages about the wilderness. Biblical characters and all that they went through became real. Jesus' spending forty days and nights with no food. Thousands of migrating Israelites needing water from a rock, manna on the grass, fowl from the sky. I thought of Hagar, banished to the wilderness, and now she had a face. It was the face of a nineteen-year-old pregnant girl carrying a shabby blanket.

On the way back to town, we passed by the border station. A scuffle was taking place around a van that had been stopped, and some US Border Patrol officers had gathered. We walked over to see what was going on. One of the officers waved to Mark and greeted us. He seemed to want a break from the activity. And he seemed sad. I noticed his eyes welling up. "Tell them to stop bringing their kids," he said to us. He was talking about the migrants.

The hardest part of his job, the officer said, was finding the remains of a child. He had found a small shoe recently.

My insides shriveled. I've always had empathy. But the image of wandering teenagers who've been deceived and the thought of bodies turning up in the desert on both sides of the border—I couldn't imagine that reality. We would learn that along the border are morgues filled with bodies whose families may never know they are there.

Clare reflected on the moment with the officer. "His tenderness—that was striking," she said. "He says to tell migrants not to bring their kids. Well, you want to tell him, 'The whole reason they're coming is *because* of their kids.'"

Mark Stephen Adams had led immersion experiences like ours for nearly ten years. It was part of his work with Frontera de Cristo, a joint ministry founded by Presbyterians on both sides of the border—the Presbyterian Church USA, and the Presbyterian Church of Mexico. The work gave Mark and his colleagues on both sides a unique view of migrant life. And because they saw so much firsthand, their insights were valuable to a lot of people. Including one named John McCain, Republican senator from Arizona. Mark met regularly with McCain's staff over the years, but never with the senator himself. Until one day in 2005.

From time to time in our history, for various reasons, immigration becomes a forefront political issue. It happened again after September 11, 2001. With the World Trade Center attacks, immigrants of every kind were viewed with suspicion. A migrant family may have been neighbors for decades with people who suddenly saw them as strange—and a threat. In the year after 9/11, hate crimes increased sixteenfold.

John McCain was sensitive to that, as a leader in a border state. A lot of good, hardworking people in Arizona were having their lives forced even farther into the shadows. So McCain decided to take the lead on immigration reform. He made it a point to join with somebody across the Senate aisle—Democratic senator Ted Kennedy of Massachusetts—to come up with a bill that would be sensible and bipartisan. They put forward the Secure America and Orderly Immigration Act. It was considered landmark legislation because it addressed the three big issues everyone was concerned about: border enforcement, guest-worker visas, and legalization leading to citizenship.

Mark knew it was a hot piece of legislation at the time. He didn't know how hot until he sat down across from McCain in the senator's office.

"My friend, you represent the church," McCain began.

It wasn't a warm tone. Mark felt his pulse quicken.

"So tell me—where is the church's voice for the immigrant?" the senator demanded. Here was the legendary McCain passion that Mark had heard about. Suddenly he knew what it was like to be in John McCain's crosshairs. There was a broad oak desk between them, but Mark felt like the senator had jumped onto it and was jabbing a finger in his chest.

"Aren't you supposed to be a friend to the foreigner?" McCain pressed him. "Aren't you supposed to raise up their voices, to take up their cause alongside them?"

Mark thought he was doing that. He was raising awareness through border immersion experiences. To the senator, aware-ness wasn't enough. People's lives were at stake.

"I'm trying to get this legislation through," he said, slapping his desk. "And I'm getting calls twenty-to-one *against* it. *Twenty to one!*" The bill was humane, it was practical, it worked across aisles, he said, so why weren't people of faith getting behind it? Instead, it was being dismissed, while good people suffered because nothing was getting done. Why weren't Christians say-ing anything? Why didn't they stand up?

It left an impression on Mark. He realized the church was very good at helping people "on the ground" with practical things. But where was the church when it came to raising our voice with immigrants in public, to stand with them?

Mark had to admit: except for the voices of grassroots faith groups and smaller denominations, Christians mainly were silent. The world was calling us out on it. We had to stand up or shut up.

CHAPTER 2

Steel Beams and a Piece of Paper

> *Every moment of our human life is a moment of*
> *crisis; for at every moment we are called upon to*
> *make an all-important decision—to choose between*
> *the way that leads to death and spiritual darkness*
> *and the way that leads towards light and life; between*
> *interests exclusively temporal and the eternal order;*
> *between our personal will . . . and the will of God.*
>
> —ALDOUS HUXLEY, *The Perennial Philosophy*

The Migrant Resource Center is an amazing place. In Agua Prieta, Mexico, near the US port of entry, it exists to serve migrants, including those who've been deported after trying to cross into the US. I hoped the teenage travelers stopped there.

"Let's consider some Bible passages," Mark said to our group. "These are God's words to his people over several millennia, and they're all about the stranger in our midst. See whether a kind of picture forms for you."

From Leviticus. "The foreigner residing among you must be treated as your native-born."

From Jeremiah. "Do what is just and right. . . . Do no wrong or violence to the foreigner, the fatherless or the widow."

From Deuteronomy. "Bring all the tithes of that year's produce and store it . . . so that . . . the foreigners, the fatherless and the widows who live in your towns may come and eat and be satisfied."

From Ezekiel. "You are to consider them as native-born . . . along with you they are to be allotted an inheritance among the tribes of Israel."

Mark set the Bible down. We sat with what we had heard.

Treat foreigners like they're native born. Do what is just and right to them. Give them food and let them eat until they're satisfied. And give them an inheritance of what you have! Justice and compassion. But generosity too. And sacrifice. Those truths weren't surprising to me about God. But they contrasted with what I heard in the news about "aliens."

"These passages aren't from one period in Israel's history," Mark pointed out. "They span all eras. And they spill over into the New Testament."

He flipped pages leftward. "You might hear a lot of people quoting Romans 13 about respecting the law and not breaking it," he said. "But there's a deep and clear context to that chapter. In the chapters on either side of it, Paul is writing to the Romans about loving others, doing justice, and practicing hospitality."

Mark read aloud Romans 12:13 (NLT): "'Always be eager to practice hospitality.' Hospitality. We don't think of it the way the ancients did," he said. "The Greek word Paul uses for 'hospitality' here says everything. It's a combination of two Greek words. *Philo,* which means brotherly love. And *xenia,* which means stranger."

I saw Clare nodding.

"If you're wondering, the answer is yes—*xeno* is the root of *xenophobia,*" Mark said. "Fear of the stranger. God is telling us to do the opposite with strangers—*philoxenia.* Don't fear the stranger—love them. Feed them. Let them share in our inheritance."

Hospitality—it's not about having our neighbors over. It's about inviting the stranger, the foreigner, the person who's vulnerable in a strange land. God wants them to know they're loved. This was pretty straightforward.

"God's heart never changes toward the foreigner, from one era to another," Mark pointed out. "We change toward the stranger," he said, "but God doesn't."

Some of my equilibrium returned when we went to climb the wall. The Border Patrol let Mark's teams try it on occasion. It was one more window into the migrant world.

I was up for it. Yet when I stared up, taking in how high those rust-colored beams rose, I realized the fear confronting anyone who tried. I would have help at the top—an immersion staffer was there waiting for me—and safe arms below if I happened to lose my grip. Not so for a migrant.

"Go, Sarah!" I had a cheering section.

The metal was cold. February cold. So cold it was hard to get a decent grasp on the beam. I hiked myself up and started.

Within a few minutes, the wind kicked up and I felt myself sway. The iron's sharp edges cut into my palms.

"Come on, Sarah!"

How did I ever think the border wall was just a fence? That you could walk up and hop over it?

A few feet higher, my hand began to bleed. My fingers grew stiff with cold. I wondered if I might fall.

But someone desperate wouldn't quit. A mother wouldn't. No parent would if it was for their child's sake.

The staffer above me reached down. Below, more cheers. But up here—frightening. I gripped his hand and he pulled me to the top. I felt safe.

Much is made of the wall I climbed. Yet it's a very minor aspect of immigration in our country. Six out of ten "undocumented" people living in the US arrived here legally; they've simply overstayed their visas. As Clare says, that's a paperwork issue, not a threat. And most people who climb the wall like I did are the desperate poor. They're the ones most severely affected by the Illegal Immigration and Reform Act, the 1996 federal law under President Clinton meant to crack down on unofficial border crossings. That act mandated the first steel barriers, separating communities on either side of the border. As restrictions became tighter, people desperate to enter the US began crossing at more dangerous points—like the Arizona desert.

Humanitarian groups predicted this would happen and protested. They knew the reasons people crossed weren't for convenience; they were matters of life and death. Between 2000 and 2016, six thousand people died trying to cross the desert. In a single county in Arizona, Border Patrol found the remains of two thousand people. But that doesn't tell the whole story. A Texas sheriff says, "For every one we find, we're probably missing five."

None of this mattered to Betty, our tour guide at the US Border Patrol Station in Douglas. From the moment we entered the heavily militarized station, we were on alert. Dwarfed by the long, scoped rifle she brandished, we received no smile from the agent as she waved us forward, "To the weapons room."

As we followed her through the station, we noted the various ethnicities of the agents, many of them Latinx (the single term now used for all genders). Betty stopped in front of a large door, pulled out a huge ring of keys, unlocked what seemed like a dozen locks, and pushed open the heavy metal.

What we saw assaulted our senses. The walls were lined with

automatic weapons of all kinds. Assault rifles. *Grenade launchers.*
It was an artillery room.

"If you're on BP," the agent said, meaning patrol, "you get to
take out whatever weapon you want."

But . . . grenades? What for?

I noticed a wall filled with framed photos, eight by tens.
Somebody's family shots?

I looked closer. One was a group picture taken alongside a
van. Several people were lined up on their knees. Their hands
were shackled. Behind them stood Border Patrol agents with
rifles. On either side, held on leashes, were dogs.

It was a hunting photo.

"Those are the prizes they caught," Betty told me.

Uh—did I hear that right? "Ma'am, I'm confused," I said. "Do
you mean the people are the prizes?"

She grinned.

Everyone fell silent.

"So," someone finally asked, "what do you like best about
the job?"

"Tracking stuff."

Stuff.

We all knew what Betty meant. She defined it for us anyway:
"Bodies."

It was obvious she wanted to be out in the field that very
moment.

Deb cleared her throat. "So, how are the migrants treated?"

"Different every day," Betty said. "It depends on who's the
boss on duty."

Clare's face reddened. "So there's no standard protocol for
how to treat people?"

Nothing, say, to keep someone from shackling a pregnant
nineteen-year-old like a hunting trophy? The agent smiled and
shook her head.

Our final visit was to a migrant shelter for men in Agua Prieta, called Centro de Atencion Migrante Exodus. Nearby was another shelter for women and children. Many people who get deported from the US end up here, including those who've lived in the United States a long time. If they don't have relatives in Mexico— and many don't—they're on their own. Once they're handed over to the Mexican government, processed and released, they immediately become homeless.

I found this out over dinner. When our group arrived at the shelter, I was overwhelmed by all the Spanish being spoken. I knew almost none. I felt a little lost. When dinnertime came, I heard a guy speaking English who looked like a volunteer. I made a beeline to him.

"Your English is so good," I told him.

He introduced himself. "I'm Agustín." A Spanish name—but a US accent! A guy maybe thirty, with a calm demeanor.

"My family's in Nevada," he said. "I grew up there. I was deported."

Deported? "So," I ventured, "are you from the USA?"

"I thought I was. I grew up believing I was. My parents brought me when I was little. From Mexico."

Agustín's manner, his gestures, his speech—they were just like those of so many guys I knew back in the Springs. I couldn't get my head around this guy's being deported.

"I was just about to turn sixteen. I needed my birth certificate to take to the DMV." His parents told him why they didn't have one. They had wanted to give him a chance at a better life. They never imagined what their decision would ultimately mean for their son.

If he wanted, the teenage Agustín could do what the law told him: go back to Mexico and apply for a visa. But the wait for someone like him wasn't months; it was years. Like any sixteen-year-old, he wasn't ready to change the whole trajectory of his life.

I didn't believe him at first. I thought he must have committed a crime. I mean, he was married to a US citizen and he wasn't allowed in the US? Come on!

Agustín said unless he could prove he'd been abused, neglected, or abandoned, he would have had to leave. So he did what a lot of kids in his situation do. He got his diploma, learned a trade, married, had children, started a business, hired people, got involved in his community, his church.

"How many kids?"

"Three," he said. "My baby girl is ten months."

I shook my head. "How long have you been away?"

"A year," he said. That meant he was here, in Mexico, when his daughter was born.

Something passed across Agustín's eyes. He lifted his plastic cup, steadying himself. "I've never held her," he said.

He suddenly stood up and I followed him to the line for dinner—bean soup and rolls. As we filled our bowls, I couldn't stop gazing at Agustín. He wiped his eyes, looking tired.

US law says if you're deported after knowingly living in the US illegally, you're banned from applying to reenter for ten years.

When Agustín told me this, he finally broke. He brought his hands to his face and his shoulders began to heave. "I just want to hold my baby girl."

My appetite vanished.

He'd tried six times to get back to them. He'd broken bones jumping fences. He'd dehydrated. He'd been stung by scorpions and bitten by a snake. But with each attempt, he'd learned more. Next time, he said, he would make it, for his children.

I felt queasy. This couldn't be true. How had I lived for twenty-four years and not known things like this happened? It seemed impossible. My whole life I'd heard about the importance of keeping families together. All the ministries that focused on families and parenting. The countless marriage seminars held at churches.

Agustín spoke eagerly now, desperately. Someone was listening, and it seemed to build his hope.I could tell nothing was going to stop him. His tears became his determination. He was never going to quit until he was with his family.

Listening to him, I realized I had known love like this: my dad's. If my brother or sister or mom or I were ever in a situation where we couldn't get to my father, nothing would stop him from getting to us. He would do anything. I knew that about my dad from my earliest years, and it taught me something about God. The Lord's love—never ending, always pursuing, always there.

Maybe Agustín thought I would go back to my old life and pray for him and his family whenever it crossed my mind. Up to this point in the trip, I'd mostly been baffled. Now I was sickened. A document, a piece of paper, could keep loving families from being together.

I could see my parents anytime I wanted. This man wouldn't see his children for a decade. How was this possibly right?

The following year, 2011, about 200,000 people were deported from the United States. If even half of them had families here, then about half a million people in the US were forcibly separated from a loved one.

Could I ignore this? On the shuttle ride to the Tucson airport, I wrestled hard. I loved my life. I loved everything about it. But I couldn't pretend I hadn't just had my world upended.

I'd heard new things from the Bible and been given new eyes to see, and yet I wrestled. "Give to Caesar what is Caesar's," Jesus said. Obey the law, do what is right. Yet another passage kept coming to mind, one I'd learned as a kid. "'Love the Lord your God with *all* your heart and with *all* your soul and with *all* your mind.' This is the first and greatest commandment. And the second is like it: 'Love your neighbor as yourself.' All the Law and the Prophets hang on these two commandments" (Matt. 22:37–40, my emphases).

I knew the true law. It was to love.

The feeling in the pit of my stomach told me I had to obey it.

CHAPTER 3

All Our Hidden Walls

*Then Jesus said to his host, "When you give a
luncheon or dinner, do not invite your friends,
your brothers or sisters, your relatives, or your
rich neighbors; if you do, they may invite you
back and so you will be repaid. But when you
give a banquet, invite the poor, the crippled, the
lame, the blind, and you will be blessed. Although
they cannot repay you, you will be repaid at the
resurrection of the righteous."*

—LUKE 14:12–14

I wrestled for a year. Whenever I told friends I wanted to do something to help undocumented immigrants, they were puzzled. "Why would you want to do that?" most responded. "They're breaking the law."

That one concern—the law—seemed to end the conversation for them. In a way, I could understand that. I was still puzzled at how to resolve Jesus' command to give to Caesar what is Caesar's. But what churned harder in me was the second part of his command: "And give to God what is God's." What did I owe to God about Agustín? He clearly put this devoted father in my path, and I couldn't shake the experience. The policy that deported Agustín was indifferent to his family, but how could God be?

For answers, I drove an hour north to Denver as often as I could. I discovered that's where most immigration events were held. In 2010, it was still rare for evangelical churches to address immigration, but leaders who did, like Rachel Smith at Denver Community Church, provided a great start. Rachel screened films on the topic, held discussions afterward, and patiently endured all my black-and-white questions. She was a safe ear for my swirling thoughts, and I met other leaders like her with whom my struggling heart found a home.

By then I had a new job with a startup software firm in the Springs, Church Community Builder. And, thankfully, I had a boss who understood the yearning ache in me. I knew Chris Fowler from church, where he saw me happily juggle work for two pastors. I thought that was why he hired me. "No," he explained, "it was because I saw you sweeping up goldfish crackers in the childcare room. And jumpstarting an outreach to the homeless." Chris shared my concern for the overlooked and the undervalued, like messy kids and people living on the streets. When I told him about my trip to the border and the encounter with Agustín, I might have guessed that Chris would see my passion more clearly than I did—as empathy for the vulnerable.

He knew I needed to move to Denver. I was spending half my paycheck on gas in my quest to keep learning. So Chris agreed to let me cut back to half-time and work remotely so I could make the big move. In a young company like ours, that was a huge deal.

I went "full immersion," renting a room from two Mexican women on Denver's west side in an area where a lot of undocumented people live. That decision—to exist on half an income in a home where English wasn't spoken—was my final severance from the "perfect life" I was reluctant to give up. I was all in.

But what was my role? I inched closer to it as I strolled down the block of my new home.

The banner draped across a majestic old brick building read, "ESL [English as Second Language] Taught Here." Above it, the name Confluence Ministries. *I can start by helping,* I thought. Little did I know, I was about to start learning.

"There are a lot of undocumented families in the neighborhood, Sarah, and ESL is one way to help," explained Jude Del Hierro. I'd have never guessed this Denver-born man was a grandfather. Jude had the youthful demeanor of a worship leader, which he'd formerly been with the Vineyard Church in a suburb north of Denver. Like me, Jude and his wife, Cindy, had also followed a deep stirring to serve the city's vulnerable. They'd been at it for decades. "But a larger question," he continued, "is, 'What is our role as Christians with the undocumented?'"

How did he know that was exactly the conflict boiling inside me?

"Undocumented people are unprotected," Jude noted. "They won't call the police when a crime is committed against them. They're afraid of being deported. So they suffer all kinds of abuses."

Here was a twist on what I'd heard about undocumented people. Some thought of them as lawbreakers. The clearer reality is that they're vulnerable to lawbreakers.

"When you're doing outreach, you're connecting to real people with real pain," Jude said. "Love people, Sarah. Be the hands of Jesus. What do hands do? They embrace, welcome, comfort, serve."

I pondered that when I went to immigration court with Clare Twomey, my pastor friend from the border. The hearing we attended was for a Latinx man in a jumpsuit and shackles. "Where's his family?" I whispered to Clare. "They should be here."

We learned the man was from California. "People get arrested and transferred from state to state for no good reason," Clare explained, "away from their families and their legal support system. His family probably couldn't afford to come."

The man's back was to us the entire time. I just wanted to offer him a smile. When the hearing ended, a bailiff led him away. *If only his family could have been here,* I thought. *It would have made such a difference to him.*

When I met Jennifer Piper, I saw something of myself. I couldn't have told you what at the time. All I knew was, wherever Piper was, that's where I wanted to be.

Jen Piper leads the American Friends Service Committee in Denver. AFSC was started by the Quakers at the start of World War I to help civilian victims at the front battle lines in northern France. Quakers are pacifists, and their US roots in civil actions for biblical justice date back to the Underground Railroad. Piper, as she's known—affectionately by friends, respectfully by critics—leads a lot of events around Denver with undocumented people. That includes vigils and demonstrations where peaceful protesters may be dragged away by arrest. "Civil actions" is what they're called, and AFSC holds them purposefully at the center of community life. They're meant to ring a loud bell in the public square to draw attention to vulnerable people suffering injustices.

If you met Jen at one of these events, you might never pick her out as the leader. She's soft spoken and has a big, shy grin for everyone. She talks tenderly about people, including those on the opposite side of a protest. "We're all part of the same community," she says. "So how do we hold to our convictions and still embrace others who are trying to figure it out too?" Yet her stances with immigrants are iron strong.

Protests are only the public face of AFSC's work. They have

a dedicated network of volunteers who do "accompaniment"—
going with undocumented people to their court dates to be with
them as the verdicts are read. After I saw the sad California man
in immigration court, I knew what a difference accompaniment
could make. AFSC also helps people get to legal appointments
and check-in meetings at ICE facilities around Denver.

One of the most important of AFSC's crucial works is helping people in detention get released on bond. This allows them
to be with their families while their cases are being decided.
Amazingly, bond release increases their chances of winning their
cases to 80 percent.

"It's about justice," Piper says. Biblical justice, that is. There's
strictly legal justice, and then there's the kind that aligns a person's standing in society with their standing in God's eyes.

Justice. I didn't think of that word whenever I saw people
protesting; I thought only of anger. But Piper's group didn't seem
like angry people. Or so I thought. Piper disagreed.

"Anger isn't an acceptable emotion in most faith circles," she
pointed out. Especially as Christians, she said, we're taught to mute
that particular emotion. "We have to create spaces for righteous
anger," she said. She was talking about the anger that God has—
described in the Bible—when vulnerable people are treated unjustly.

I soon learned how frequently immigrants endure injustices
all around Denver. I volunteered with a community center called
El Centro Humanitario, interviewing day laborers and discover-
ing the cruel practices that take advantage of them. They would
spend a day at a job site but not be paid. When they asked for the
promised wages, they were threatened with calls to ICE. Others
were driven to rural locations to work all day and left stranded
at day's end. An undocumented man on a construction site fell
two stories from a ladder and broke his spine. The foreman was
so scared of being caught with an undocumented worker that he
jumped in his truck and sped away.

I learned about righteous anger—God's anger—in the Old Testament: "Do what is just and right. . . . Do no wrong or violence to the foreigner. . . . But if you do not obey these commands, declares the LORD, I swear by myself that this palace will become a ruin" (Jer. 22:3, 5). I also learned how Jesus connected that same anger in a New Testament setting: "They also will answer, 'Lord, when did we see you hungry or thirsty or *a stranger* or needing clothes or sick or in prison, and did not help you?' He will reply, 'Truly I tell you, whatever you did not do for one of the least of these, you did not do for me.' Then they will go away to eternal punishment, but the righteous to eternal life" (Matt. 25:44–46, my emphasis).

Nothing looked like anger in Piper. But it was there. Embodied in a shy, quiet-spoken woman. All I knew was, I saw Piper and AFSC protecting people—unafraid to stand with them in the places where injustices take place. If that was anger, I wanted to learn how to show it—Piper's way.

I never had a talent for grasping big theological concepts—like, say, eternity. When I was a kid, I asked my mom what it means. She paused to think. "Eternity is like, hmm—it's like waking up every day forever." *Forever?* Even as a six-year-old, I knew nobody does that. I went to the back yard of our home in the central Texas countryside, lay down, and looked up at the sky to try to get my mind around eternity. It made my head hurt.

I was happier listening to "Go to the Ant," Judy Rogers' song for Christian kids, exhorting them to be industrious. I could relate to that. My big brother, David, won prizes for raising chickens through Bastrop County's 4H program. He and Anna and I stayed busy with the service projects Mom devised for our church's youth group, visiting nursing homes and the humane society. When I finally got old enough to bake, I was thrilled because it meant I could serve people through food. That sent me on a great hamantash hunt, scouring the internet to find dough that wouldn't crumble out of the oven. When I succeeded, I sent my homework essay about it to my Russian Jewish grandma—Dad's mom—who lived in California: "Jews eat this sensational dessert year-round but mostly during the Purim, which commemorates the downfall of Haman. . . . My future plans are to continue baking this cookie for family, friends, the elderly, and the poor. This is the foremost self-satisfaction one can have: accomplishing something you love to do while serving others."

As Mom notes, the endpoint of everything for me was to be a nurse. Specifically, to be Florence Nightingale—the British "Lady with the Lamp" who treated all those rows of wounded soldiers and forged modern nursing. I got mad when the county library system ran out of biographies about her. "Aren't twelve books enough?" Mom pleaded, hoping to quell one of my legendary meltdowns. But real-life nursing came when I assisted our pregnant mama cat, who strained and howled and delivered a squirming, pinkened litter directly onto my lap. I looked up from this wonder to see my mother beaming.

I was her busy bee, just as she had been for her mother, my Polish Grandma, whose accent could still faintly be heard. Grandma had been shamed for it after she moved to the US as the bride of my career Air Force Grandpa. Grandma was quiet and humble but had a competitive spirit—she won every foot race against boys as she grew up—and in west Texas she became a high achiever to compensate, becoming her city's accountant. To my mom, hurt by the jokes about her mother, Grandma's job stature was a kind of quiet justice.

I didn't hear much about justice in church growing up. Now, awakened to immigrant life in Denver, I saw justice mentioned everywhere in the Bible—a term associated not with courts but with God's heart. It was about making things right for everyone, because all have equal standing in the Lord's sight.

Justice for immigrants? One immigrant was always present in my million swirling thoughts: Agustín. With every event I attended, his dilemma stayed with me. Where was justice for him? For his fatherless kids? Justice that reflected his standing in God's eyes? I wanted nothing more than to see that.

And yet I still wrestled with the same Bible passages my church friends did. Verses that were deeply embedded in my mind and heart.

One cold night, I had a revelatory moment. I woke freezing. The window in the bedroom I rented from the Mexican women wouldn't close. With winter air blasting in, I shivered under the bedcovers. Instantly, a verse popped into my head: "Love your neighbor as yourself." Why that verse, I had no idea.

But one phrase nagged at me: "as yourself."

The meaning sank in: What did *I* want right now? To be warm.

If I were hungry? Something to eat. If I had nowhere to go? A roof over my head. If I were alone and isolated? Someone to visit me.

"The entire law and all the demands of the prophets are based on these two commandments," Jesus said (Matt. 22:40 NLT): to love God, and to love our neighbors *as ourselves*.

That's the *law*, Jesus said.

A guy who heard Jesus say this looked for a legal loophole. He asked him, "And who is my neighbor?" (Luke 10:29). Jesus answered with a story about an injured stranger abandoned by the side of the road in a religious community. Every faith leader passed him by. Only a traveling Samaritan, an outsider considered to be a heretic, reached out to help. The Samaritan didn't ask where the injured man was from. He simply "took pity on him," picked him up, gave him shelter, healed his wounds, and paid for all his expenses while he recovered (vv. 30–35). Jesus made it clear who the questioner's neighbor was: anyone in desperate need. When he finished the story, he told the guy, "Go and do likewise" (v. 37).

Love God. Love your neighbor as yourself.

I don't even have those two things down, I thought. *What good is parsing all the other stuff if I don't do these?*

Shivering under the covers, I settled every biblical question I had about immigration. The law—God's law—is to love.

God had made something else very clear to me: He had brought our neighbors to our doorstep, in immigrants. He placed wounded travelers right in front of us, in a way we all could recognize.

And we can call for their justice. Jen Piper points out how US immigration policies over the past twenty years weren't designed for any practical need; they were designed to be punitive and exclusionary. They've chaotically upended the lives of undocumented people who've lived here for ten, twenty, thirty years. People like Augusín. The very people President Reagan had in mind in the 1980s when he did something remarkable: he granted amnesty to undocumented folks. The amnesty was qualified, but it was generous. A lot of people who'd been deported got to return to the country they knew as home.

Caring advocates like Piper taught me that our language about immigrants matters a lot—that they aren't to be called "illegal" but rather "undocumented"; no human being is "illegal." They aren't to be called "detainees" but are "people in detention"; they're not some*thing* to be labeled but people like the rest of us.

And they're not inferiors to be "helped" but peers to be "companioned"; we walk alongside them because we have equal standing in God's eyes.

The more I absorbed, the more something came alive in me. My theology was starting to conform to the reality I saw around me—and to words in the Bible I already knew.

I may be the least of all singers in the musically talented Jackson family. Yet when Christmas came around, I became a bona fide member of a worship team: Jude Del Hierro's. He was one of the few church leaders in Denver whose congregation had a regular ministry to people detained at the Aurora ICE Processing Center.

"Have you ever been inside there?" Jude asked.

"The detention center? No."

"You're about to go now," he said. "You're singing with us on Christmas Day."

Detention centers are notoriously secretive. My only knowledge about what happened inside Aurora ICE came from advocates. I had heard about "pods," the areas where groups of immigrants are detained, but that term didn't reveal much. On Christmas, as we set up mics and music stands, I saw that a pod is a cage. With a group shower. And an open toilet.

The Aurora ICE building is set up like a prison. Imagine a huge Walmart divided into eight equal parts. Each part makes up a pod. At the center of these pods is an octagonal guard station. As you sit at the station, you can turn in a circle and see clearly into every pod.

The big square building is bisected east and west, and north and south. One bisecting line consists of a hallway running to and from the guard station. The other bisecting line consists of long, narrow recreational "yards" on either side of the guard station. A rec yard normally is made of grass and needs sunshine. But the "rec yards" in Aurora ICE don't get sunshine—and don't need it: the ground is concrete. These rec areas don't get enough fresh air either. The ceiling is fifteen or twenty feet high, with a two-foot opening between it and the walls that support it; outside air has to trickle down to the rec area. There's no way to look outside to the living world because all the windows in the building are covered or blacked out. The small two-foot gap at the top of the rec-yard wall provides the only outside view. You can see only inches of light from the sky.

What I saw that Christmas Day affected me deeply. As we sang beautiful carols, I saw despair on faces I hadn't expected to see: African, Asian, Balkan, Russian, Scandinavian. There were Latin Americans too, but so many Africans! I'd thought people in detention were mainly Mexican.

A few people knew the songs we sang. But our services were only in English and Spanish, so some were left to nod their heads or clap or just sit still. For those of no religious faith, I'm sure attending the service was just something to do. The place felt so very desolate.

And then, not long after we exited the building, I heard two words that changed everything.

I was standing on an icy sidewalk where I'd joined so many of Piper's vigils, and I overheard a guy mention El Refugio.

"The Refuge?" I asked. "What's that?"

"It's a hospitality home in Georgia. Like the Ronald McDonald House, but for immigrant families," the guy said. "It sits right next to the biggest detention center in America."

I felt a buzzing inside me. *Hospitality.* "What do they do there?"

"They help families reunite with their loved ones in the prison."

"How?"

"A lot of detained people are a long way from their families. And their loved ones can't afford a trip to visit them. El Refugio gives them a place to stay for free." I thought of the lonely man in court from California.

"A hospitality home. Is there anything like that in Denver?"

"There aren't too many anywhere," the guy said. "Most are in the border states, close to where people cross over. Some bigger cities too. But El Refugio is the only one I know about."

Time stopped. All the noisy, furious rods cranking through my head for so long instantly clicked into gear.

I pictured all of the despairing faces in the pods at Christmas. What would it mean for them to have their families visit them?

All I have to do is get a home. Then open it up. Then let people stay with me. Eat a meal together and make up their bed. Yes!

After all my searching, all my learning, I finally knew my role. I could barely wait to go online and check out—what was it?—El Refugio. Once I did, I knew I'd see my future. I had to go visit those folks to see how they do it.

This was going to be so easy!

PART 2

Doors To Open

Blessed are they who do not theorize about heavenly things. Blessed are they who keep to the way that is shown them, whatever life brings.

—CHRISTOPH FRIEDRICH BLUMHARDT, *Action in Waiting*

CHAPTER 4

Bring Peace

At first sight, the situation of this world suggests despair. For Christians, however, the last word is always hope. Despite everything, we have no use for a misleading or alienating hope that looks only to eternal life—as though eternity didn't start here and now, because it is here and now that we build an eternal life.

—Dom Helder Camara, 1972 speech, "The Degradation of the Worlds and the Renovation of the Earth"

On Thur, Dec 29, 2011 at 11:54 AM, Sarah Jackson wrote:

Hey, Anton!

Really looking forward to coming down to El Refugio in a few days. Question for ya—which city do you live in? Also, which is the nearest big city next to you?

Reason I'm asking is because I'm a salsa dancer and whenever I travel, I like to see if there's a place I can dance. I probably won't have any time to dance, but just thought I'd ask.

Thanks, Sarah

On Thur, Dec 29, 2011 at 7:35 PM, Anton Flores wrote:

We live in the small town of LaGrange—pop. 30,000. Sorry, no salsa clubs here. Stewart Detention Center is in the itty-bitty town of Lumpkin—pop. 1,300 with hundreds of salsa dancers, unfortunately detained.

Most people in advocacy work have a sense of humor. You kind of have to. Anton Flores-Maisonet's humor is always in place, and he's got great timing. Anton might've just been feeling me out with his joke about salsa dancing. If so, I understand why. "We do tend to get a lot of idealistic young people," he told me later.

"Advocate" is too light a description for Anton. He has three gears: gentle, reflective pastor; piercing, fire-breathing prophet; life-loving family man and faithful companion who's always ready with the humor. Some people just seem to have it all figured out. When I met Anton, I knew I'd picked the right mentor.

All of these traits came out in equal measure on the drive from Atlanta's airport to the Stewart Detention Center, two hours southwest. "Yes, come up and stay with my family," he answered my first Facebook message. "Spend time with us and learn how we do things." I'd written that I wanted to pirate his idea for El Refugio. He answered with an itinerary for my visit over a four-day weekend. I noticed that each day would hold something different—great for the thorough learning experience I wanted. Yet two items recurred each day: "visit detained immigrants" and "serve at El Refugio." Obvious priorities.

It had bothered me a little that Anton took forty-eight hours to answer my first message. I had to sort of harass him till he did. Every "good practice" I'd absorbed in large church life and business told me to respond quickly to inquiries.

"We're more values driven than policy driven," he said casually. "Values driven"—a phrase that often signaled a disorganized nonprofit run by ministry-minded people. Not the case with

Anton. It revealed clearly what—and who—got his attention. He steered everything back to immigrants.

Anton was one of those college professors you loved as a student because he embodied what he taught. He's also an intent listener. I imagined every class with him at LaGrange College, a Methodist school, as a deep life lesson. His subjects and passions—theology and social work—were one thing. (Faith *is* action—*yes!*) I pictured those passions seeping from every pore in his lectures. His passion had led him to give up his tenure-track job and start an intentional community alongside his wife, Charlotte, and another couple, Norma and Arturo, that included Latin American neighbors. For all four, this was simply living out the gospel.

It didn't take long for Anton to see the day-to-day struggles of immigrants. Their struggles heightened when police began doing relentless traffic stops to check driver's licenses. In a single year, the police set up 190 roadblocks in little LaGrange—more than one every other day. The tickets they issued for driving without a license were $500, and late payment would increase the amount to $800. It was a targeted practice against a specific population: undocumented people. Anton estimated it brought in $125,000 a year for the small town—all on the backs of people who had a hard time making a living to begin with. Officials knew undocumented people couldn't fight back.

It was here, from Anton, that I learned what people went through in some countries—the random brutality of a gang-corrupted government, the crimes and murders never pursued. It's one reason why some came to the United States. Once they got here, many were victimized in a different way, like traffic stops. Their government back home didn't protect them; why would our government be any different? They weren't used to having somebody stand with them.

But Anton did. He accompanied them to traffic court. He

raised money to pay the tickets. On those days in court, Anton boiled as he listened to the judge scapegoat his close neighbors, calling them untrustworthy liars for using false documents to get jobs. Anton knew those false documents were required by unscrupulous employers. Those employers, in a panic, had heavily recruited Latin American workers to meet construction deadlines for the 1996 Olympics in Atlanta. Once the deadlines were met, the workers were cast off, and condemned for being in the US.

The police roadblocks in LaGrange eventually made national news. A reporter for the *Los Angeles Times* launched an investigation, which unveiled criminal practices by businesses exploiting immigrant families.

Physically, I stood eye to eye with Anton, but I knew right away the size of this guy's soul made his presence huge. He stood tallest at the entryway to the Stewart Detention Center, where he led demonstrations. "The population inside the facility is bigger than the town's," Anton told me. Eighteen hundred people in detention, and only 1,300 citizens in Lumpkin. The detention center was a big employer in a small town, so there wasn't much sympathy for Anton's demonstrations.

"What is America's biggest immigrant detention center doing isolated in southwest Georgia?" I asked as Anton drove south along US Highway 27. "I thought most immigrants are in cities."

"More than half of immigrant detention centers are in rural areas," he said. He pointed out how hard it was for immigration lawyers to visit their clients at the Stewart facility. Most worked in Atlanta. "Over two hours away, and it eats up their whole day. It's not like they have only one client," he said. "A lawyer might have to hang around all day in the waiting room. It all happens at ICE's discretion."

No sooner do you enter Lumpkin's town limits than the looming Stewart Detention Center appears. It's far bigger than the Aurora ICE facility, and that's saying something.

Anton cut the engine at the curb outside the facility. I assumed he wanted to show me around, so I followed him out of the car. But as we walked toward the gate, he handed me a scrap of paper. On it was scribbled a Spanish name and some numbers.

"So," I asked, "are we going to hold a prayer vigil for this guy out here?"

"No," Anton said, "that's who you're going to visit inside." He saw my surprise. "You okay with it?" he asked casually.

"Sure, of course," I stammered. I had sung with Jude inside Aurora ICE, but I'd never been inside a prison to visit someone.

Trailing Anton, I was ushered through a security gate, surrendering my driver's license, phone, pen and pad, and everything else except for what I wore. The lobby was a lot like the one back in Aurora: pretty nondescript. The unsmiling guards who manned the place made eye contact only to size us up. I looked around at the handful of people in the waiting room, mostly women, some with kids. It was weighted with the same desolate sadness as the pods in Aurora ICE.

We were led to a guard station next to the metal-detector entrance. Anton gave me no instructions, no preparation, nada. A few minutes later, I found myself seated in a booth with a telephone—just like in prison movies—facing a Latinx guy through dim plexiglass. He might have been in his twenties, and I gulped at the thought that I might not be able to communicate with him. The telephone line had a scratchy noise that broke up our voices.

"Hola?" I ventured, assuming he was a Spanish speaker.

"Hola," the guy answered back, smiling.

And so we talked. He graciously accommodated my Spanglish.

What did we talk about?

Soccer. Siblings. What we did on holidays. I won't lie, it was a little awkward. There were a few stretches of silence. At one point I think I told him about my recent breakup with a guy. He ended up encouraging me! "Don't be sad," he said, forming a fist, "stay strong."

Before I knew it, the hour had passed. In that short time, I learned that he had been locked up here for several months. He hadn't seen anyone he knew because he didn't have relatives nearby. "Thank you for coming to visit me," he said, genuinely grateful, as we rose from our stools. "My head was in a different place an hour ago."

I could only guess what he meant. All I knew was that I hadn't done anything. Yet it had done something for him.

"How was the visit?" Anton asked on the way out.

"I guess it was—okay?" I described the conversation.

"Someone in the world cared about him," Anton said. That opened my eyes. Nothing in the guy's incarcerated existence told him he was worth anything.

"So how did you get his name?" I asked Anton.

"Detained people can request visits," he said. "But not many loved ones can come all the way out here. You can imagine how many folks inside never see a single soul."

And that was the reason for El Refugio, he said. It was to bring hope to people inside by visits from their families. "It keeps them going," Anton said. "But even a visit from a stranger means something." He smiled. "Maybe especially a stranger."

I loved that he used that word—stranger! It reminded me of a favorite verse: "Do not forget to entertain strangers, for by so doing some have unwittingly entertained angels" (Heb. 13:2 NKJV). I loved the idea that hospitality—love of the stranger—brings heaven down to us.

The hospitality home—El Refugio—was just a mile or so away from the Stewart Detention Center. Anton prepared me for the visiting family staying there. "You understand why they're so frazzled when they arrive," he said. "Everything is a scramble for them just to get here. They have to find money for a trip across several states. Once they arrive, they have to hurry to the detention center for visiting hours. It's all-out stress for them."

Anton parked in front of a small yellow house. Classic postwar wood frame, white trim, thin wrought-iron railing on the porch. The Refuge.

Inside, two women sat at the kitchen table having tea. One was Latinx, the other white. Nearby, on the floor of a simply but warmly furnished living room, three kids quietly played a board game. It was a picture of calm, a world away from the weariness I saw in the detention-center lobby.

"Hello," the white woman greeted us. The Latinx mom smiled and nodded.

"Sarah, this is Amy Edwards," Anton said, gesturing to the volunteer. "She and her husband, P.J., help run El Refugio."

He whispered to me, "These kids just got to visit their dad." They looked calm, like the mom, as they played. "This is the first moment of peace they've had on their trip," he added.

Anton encouraged me to nose around while he caught up with the two women. I thumbed through some fliers on a table in the living room. On top was one titled "Father's Day Campaign." Just below the title was a request:

Help us send a card or letter to people detained at Stewart Detention Center on Father's Day.

El Refugio is collecting handwritten cards from people like you to send to detained immigrants at Stewart Detention Center. We know that for detained fathers, this is a difficult holiday, spent separated from their children and loved ones. With your help, we can send a message of solidarity and hope to fathers and help to alleviate their isolation.

Fifteen minutes of your time can help make someone's day!

I made a note of this—*cards and letters, yes!* They would go a long way for the lonely people I'd seen in detention.

I flipped over the flier. The back side gave instructions on how to write a message of hope, in English, Spanish, French, and Somali. I made another note to myself: *All kinds of languages needed.*

Another flier, titled "Families Need Our Support":

The waiting room at Stewart Detention Center is filled with families who have traveled long distances to visit someone they love. The process is slow. The guard informs a woman she cannot visit her husband. Why? Because of the holes in her jeans.

An El Refugio volunteer is in the waiting room, and she keeps extra clothing in her car. She gives the woman a pair of pants. The woman is granted a visit with her husband.

Visiting a loved one at Stewart Detention Center is stressful and confusing. For those detained inside Stewart, life is harrowing. As many as 1,800 immigrants are detained at any given time. Some are sick and deprived of medical care. Others have been further isolated as punishment, even while trying to follow Stewart's arbitrary rules.

Your gift to El Refugio eases the plight of families who have been separated by cruel immigration policies.

Incredible! How did a volunteer know to have extra clothes on hand? Who would think of that?

Experience, I realized. And bad experiences. A frantic visitor's trip was rescued by someone on hand ready to help.

Another flier on the table looked like an invitation. It was a sad one: "Vigil for Roberto Medina-Martinez Saturday, January 15, 5 p.m., Stewart Detention Center: Join us for a gathering to remember Roberto and all those who have died in detention."

I turned over the card and read about the man who had died. I learned that in fifteen years, 184 people had died in immigrant detention. Whoa—a person has died in US immigration custody *every month* for more than a decade and a half?

I glanced up at Anton. He shared a gentle laugh with the mom and the volunteer. *They deal with so much heartache here,* I thought. *And yet this house is so full of peace.*

Lying next to the fliers was an information sheet about El Refugio. It described their basic services to families: a free place to stay, meals, and accompaniment when they go to visit loved ones in detention. The final paragraph struck me hard: "We can listen. At night, over dinner and long after the dishes have been cleared, visiting families share their stories. The room fills with anguish, but afterward there is palpable relief. There is comfort in knowing they are not alone, that other wives, sons, daughters, sisters, brothers, mothers, and fathers are walking the same confusing path. At El Refugio, we are here to walk that path alongside anyone who needs our support."

I didn't have to take notes for that. A picture was emerging of what this place was all about. *So this is a hospitality home.* That word, I realized—*hospitality*—shares the same root as *hospital.* Both are places of healing.

One of the first known hospitals in the world was built for vulnerable people, and particularly for immigrants. Basil, the bishop of Caesarea, founded it in the fourth century for orphans, widows, the poor, and especially for impoverished strangers. Hospitals were societies' culmination of a humble practice that took place in virtually every Christian home since the church's earliest days. Marcella, Fabiola, Melania and others most associated with Christian hospitality weren't what we might imagine, rich ladies who spread lavish dinner tables. Some of them gave away all their families' wealth to care for strangers.

Every major religion practiced a form of hospitality, caring for the stranger. For Christians, it was about more than charity. It was a living picture of the kingdom of heaven that Jesus preached. The hospitality table, where every person's status is leveled by the need for sustenance, was a sign of hope. It told the vulnerable stranger, "Things don't have to be as they are. Injustice doesn't have to rule your life. People care for you, and they're sent by a God who loves you."

Hospitality was so crucial to the early church's credibility that it became a prerequisite for church leadership. Ministers like John Wesley railed whenever the practice was misused to gain social standing instead of to benefit the vulnerable. The Benedictines, a Catholic order founded specifically to welcome strangers, have excelled at it for fifteen centuries.

The practitioners I sat with for dinner that night in LaGrange, Georgia, fit perfectly into this glorious historical stream. They made me feel like family. Anton and Charlotte had invited Norma and Arturo, cofounders of the Alterna Community, to spend time talking about their beginnings.

The Alterna community in their Latin American neighborhood was just a year old in 2007 when Anton first heard what really went on inside the Stewart Detention Center in Lumpkin. A hunger strike was taking place, and Anton poked around to find out what it was about. He learned about the horrible conditions in Stewart, from medical neglect to what amounted to inhumane conditions.

Detained people were being used to maintain the facility, including cooking and cleaning, for a-dollar-a-day wages. To make things worse for the people suffering inside, almost nobody won their case. Ninety-seven out of every hundred people at the Stewart facility were deported. That's way higher than in the rest of the country. The environment inside Stewart was so oppressive and unhealthy that people detained there lost hope. Their spirits withered, and so did their bodies. Some died from untreated sickness. Several died by suicide.

Anton decided to lead a demonstration in front of the facility. Later acts of nonviolent civil disobedience—meaning he would be arrested—were the only way to draw attention to the situation. And they did. The ACLU investigated. They named the Stewart facility and three other ICE detention centers as "consistently [showing] that [ICE] is incapable of protecting the basic human rights of immigrants under its care."

"We started to hear from families in North and South Carolina, looking for help," Anton said. "A lot of the people detained in those states are sent to Stewart, but ICE makes it incredibly hard for people to find out where their loved one is detained. Those families didn't push back, so we helped them find out where their loved one was. If they were in Stewart, we offered to drive down to Lumpkin with them, to accompany them on a visit. We knew they would get just one hour for that visit. Afterward, the moms and kids came out looking crushed and defeated."

Gathering volunteers, Anton proposed they rent a house down in Lumpkin to host those out-of-town families overnight. That's how El Refugio began. Families drove in for the weekend and were able to stay in a place for free. That allowed them to extend their visits. Alterna of volunteers rotated staying in the house to host them.

"So that's El Refugio," Anton said, scraping his dinner plate. "How about you, Sarah? Tell us about your vision."

Vision? "It's more like a month-old idea," I told them. "I'm flying by the seat of my pants." I'd learned more at El Refugio in one day than I could've dreamed up in years.

Anton's smile is part delight and part cunning. It draws you in as if he has a secret to share, something he already knows you need. When I saw it curl across his face, I knew he and Charlotte and Norma and Arturo had plenty to share with me. And so we all went late into the night talking about our experiences, venting and laughing, exchanging ideas.

There was joy around the table. Yet most of the stories these warm, wonderful people told me were hard ones. I caught myself wondering, How could these heavy stories be so invigorating? And how could these sensitive people keep their joy through all the things they described?

It was the telling that brought peace, I realized. That's what the flier meant: "The room fills with anguish, but afterward there is palpable relief."

I knew that anyone who entered the doors of this home—or at El Refugio—felt peace as I did. I glanced over at the two Flores boys, playing a video game. Jairo, their adopted son from Guatemala; Eli, the younger, tender artist and writer. Despite the realities their parents faced every day, the family was enveloped in peace. At one point, Eli looked up and offered, "Dad, Sarah can have my room."

Charlotte put on the tea kettle. Anton said, "You've probably heard the saying, 'No justice, no peace.' I think there's something better. 'Where there's no justice, *bring* peace.'"

I'd seen him doing that all day long.

It suddenly struck me that I had been in Denver just a few hours earlier. It had been a long day, but just my kind. I must have looked a little forlorn when it ended.

"Sorry about the salsa," Anton discerned. "But we do have 'Just Dance 3' on Wii." Jairo and Eli were great partners for me. Together we danced well into the night.

Each day I was there went this way: Visit detained immigrants. Serve at El Refugio. Both tasks meant meeting beautiful people crushed by circumstances the world had cast on them. I thought I started to understand a little better Jesus' words, "You visited *me* in prison." We were God's eyes and ears, witnessing and listening to broken, abandoned people mostly forgotten by a world that hid them in detention. I found myself getting better at conversation with the people I visited through the plexiglass.

Back at El Refugio, I made copies of all the fliers and cards. I watched how the house was run by the volunteers, and I took notes like crazy. I witnessed a minor feud between two volunteers over which side of the sink the towel holder should go on. Anton smiled his bemused smile over that one. And every day, I was forming a blueprint. What systems I would put in place, how I would organize things. The thought of doing this—a hospitality home—was becoming clearer, sharper. My enthusiasm must have shown because again Anton seemed to read my thoughts.

"Sarah," he said late one night over tea, after everyone was asleep, "I think you need to be willing to rethink some things about what you believe. In fact, maybe everything you know about God."

Ooooh-kay . . . I thought I'd already been doing that—for two years! I'd rethought *everything* since my border trip. Anton seemed to know something more.

"I'm talking about the triumphalism we learned in church," he said.

He told me about the influences that gave him his calling. One of the most profound was a Catholic hospitality home called New Hope House, a ministry of mercy to people on death row and their loved ones. "They shaped and formed my ideas," Anton said. Shaped by ministry on death row—I couldn't imagine that.

"Be willing to suffer with people," he told me. "To be vulnerable to suffering. To be exposed to very dark realities. Remember, 'Nonetheless the sparrow doesn't fall to the ground without God seeing it.' That's one thing we're doing here. We're witnesses, and that's important. It encourages anyone to know their story is heard, that their anguish is seen and known. We're standing with people against the evil done to them and raising our voices over their injustice. Standing and speaking up is one thing. But it's another to walk alongside a person in the worst time of their life."

Words echoed back to me—Jude Del Hierro's words: "Outreach to real people comes with real pain." I saw why Anton had thrown me into the deep end that first day, visiting the guy in detention. All of this was about nothing more or less than simple, human connection.

"You have a vision," Anton affirmed. "But before you try sharing it with people, embody it. Live it, incarnate it. If you try to convince people to join you in something, don't fire them up with talk. Live out your mission. And do it unapologetically."

He sipped his tea as I absorbed this. "All we're doing is reminding people they have and deserve basic human dignity," he said. "Others will see that, and they'll be drawn to you without fully knowing why. They'll want to be part of it."

I'd seen how it was done. I knew firsthand what a home like El Refugio could mean for people.

This is something I was made for, I thought.

I didn't know then how hard it would be to find a house to do this kind of work in Denver. But I did know one thing from my time in LaGrange, Georgia. It was the name I would give that work: Casa de Paz. "House of Peace."

CHAPTER 5

The Nine-Foot Burrito

*Keeping people in a refugee camp is punishing
people who have committed no crime except trying
to save their own lives and the lives of their loved
ones. . . . The camp is the place where we keep
those who we do not see as being fully human.*

—VIET THAN NGUYEN, *The Displaced*

All you want to do is find a house that's cheap to rent. A place to
provide some simple shelter and hospitality for visitors. A kind of
Ronald McDonald House for families journeying through immigrant detention.

If that's your one mission—to find a house so you can provide
those things—it's best not to start during a housing crisis. When
I got back from El Refugio, Denver rents were skyrocketing.

Every afternoon that winter, after wrapping up work for
Church Community Builder, I crisscrossed the city in my hatch-
back chasing rare ads for house rentals. By the time I arrived at
each place, it had been snapped up. That was frustrating, but the
truth is, all of those places were dumps. I pride myself on being
able to rough it in just about any space, but some of the places

were unlivable. No way would I put up a vulnerable family in one. A decent house was out of the question.

Searching for an apartment was just as desperate. What owner would want to rent to someone with my purpose? "Yes, I'd love to take this apartment. By the way, I'll be running an immigrant hotel out of it. Every day, your tenants will see a different family of a different nationality coming and going through my door. They won't mind, will they?"

I dreaded making that big reveal as I sat across from the leasing manager at an apartment building in Aurora. Kim was a white woman about ten or fifteen years older than me. She was friendly but no-nonsense, the kind of sizer-up who's good at managing a place in a rough neighborhood. I knew the area's reputation for open drug deals, sex trafficking, and the occasional gunshot. But I had to look there; it was one of the few areas I could afford the rent. And, coincidentally, just across busy Peoria Drive from the apartment building was the Aurora ICE Processing Center.

As I worked up to the big topic, I asked Kim every question I could muster about lease terms, rent escalation, parking, laundry facilities—just stalling. I had been turned down every day for weeks. Kim could tell I was sitting on something, and because she'd been doing this for years, she pressed me with questions of her own. Finally, I gave it to her straight.

"I want to rent this place so I can take in people from out of town," I said, clearing my throat. "I want to host families who come here to visit a loved one in immigrant detention."

Kim was silent. I couldn't have ever guessed the thoughts I had just triggered in her.

Two decades earlier, in her twenties, she'd been in love with an undocumented guy she was dating. They were on a cross-country trip to visit his family, driving through Washington state's beautiful national forests. Her boyfriend had grown up in that region with his aunt, brother, and sister, all from Mexico.

He was so little when his parents brought him to the US that he barely remembered anything about it. Now his parents were back in Mexico permanently, having been deported.

He and Kim were driving just north of Spokane when they pulled aside for a scenic view. Neither realized they were three miles from the Canadian border and that Border Patrol regularly checked identification on anyone in the area. A BP vehicle pulled up next to theirs and an officer asked to see their identification. When the officer discovered Kim's boyfriend's status, he arrested him.

Sitting with me in the leasing office, Kim remembered how that moment utterly destroyed her boyfriend's life. He had lived in the US for almost two decades, but in a single moment he'd lost everything: his house, his car, his career. He spent five months in immigrant detention and was deported.

It shattered Kim. Every hope she had about her future disappeared with the sight of her boyfriend being shoved into the back seat of that Border Patrol car.

Kim opened a drawer in her desk in the leasing office. "People should have the right to feel safe and free," she said calmly. She pulled out a set of keys. "Go take a look at this unit. It would be great to have you here."

Two golden keys slid toward me across her desk. They glow in my memory like a miracle. The odds were stacked against my ever finding a decent home in Denver for Casa de Paz and the families I wanted to host. But that day I was blessed to encounter someone with a small measure of authority—somebody who could do something and who did because she empathized.

Looking back, I realize it wasn't a miracle at all. A person like Kim isn't unusual, but her willingness to go out of her comfort zone was. Everyone in the US is touched by an immigrant's life in some way. We're just a single degree of separation from them. And Kim's decision revealed a lasting truth to me: all it takes is knowing one immigrant—someone more like you than you think—and it changes everything for you.

I went straight from the leasing office into the courtyard and heard my steps echo up the wrought-iron stairs to my new home. Kim said the bedroom window looked across Peoria Drive, directly at Aurora ICE. I strode straight to the bedroom. I wanted to look out from my 625-square-foot hospitality home onto the 15,000-square-foot human warehouse where I had stood protesting with advocates every month for the past year.

There, in view from the second floor, sat the behemoth building, hulking and nondescript, the size of six football fields inside. It was hidden from Peoria's heavy traffic by a long strip of stores anchored by a tire shop and a bodega. Most people in Denver didn't know a federal detention center was in its midst, a windowless, gray declaration of how we treat people who are just like us but don't have documents. The same is true in any American city: most people never realize there's an immigrant detention facility near them. That has to be by design. It's something we don't want to look at. Maybe because it would make us look at ourselves.

I wasn't done protesting, I told myself. I would just do it another way. I would help restore lifelines of love between people separated by detention.

⌐

Renting the apartment was a lot easier to do because of Denver's Mennonites. Like the Quakers, Mennos, as they casually call each other, have a long heritage of standing up for their biblical convictions—especially on behalf of the vulnerable—at great personal sacrifice. They're especially serious about honoring the commandment not to kill, so much so that they won't fight even to defend their own lives. It's why over centuries they migrated from region to region whenever they were persecuted, rather than fight. Yet they'll put themselves in harm's way to protect others. The Mennonites were the first group in the US to write a formal protest against slavery.

When a church denomination has that kind of sacrificial legacy, it tends to last from generation to generation. It was no surprise that Denver's Mennos would advocate for immigrants, documented or otherwise. I'd gotten to know a few through Jen Piper's AFSC protests outside of Aurora ICE. That's where I met the pastor of First Mennonite Church in Denver. He'd heard about my vision, and one evening outside of ICE, he handed me an envelope. "This is for your rent," Vern Rempel said. "It should cover three months."

I remember gulping. Not just because it was so generous a gift but because, once again, *this was becoming real*. Vern's gesture told me that a body of people were depending on me to follow through—people with convictions of their own, bred through centuries of sacrificial service. The envelope shored up my confidence, but it was also unnerving. I knew I couldn't turn back now if I wanted to.

⁓

"So what are you doing on a beautiful spring Friday afternoon?" Jude's voicemail came a couple of months after I moved into the apartment. "You'll never guess who wants to meet for lunch," he said. "The warden from Aurora ICE."

That led to the nine-foot burrito. Only Jude, a lifelong Denverite, would know a place that catered that kind of novelty. I sat at Confluence Ministries' kitchen table across from the warden and his bespectacled young assistant, two surprisingly friendly men. As we talked, I saw that both guys had genuine compassion for the people under their watch. That puzzled me a little. I wondered how anyone could stay tenderhearted while running a detention prison like the one I had encountered in Georgia.

"Tell them about your vision, Sarah," Jude said.

I gave a quick elevator speech and surprised myself at how sharp my vision had become after the visit to El Refugio. I told them about visiting the lonely young man in detention and how I saw his burden lift. They were intrigued.

"A lot of people could use those visits," the warden said. "Yes," his assistant agreed, adjusting his glasses. "They can sink low pretty fast."

The warden offered an idea. "Let's get you in as a volunteer to teach ESL. Even a little English is a huge help to people. When you run the class, you can tell them about your hospitality home. Then they can tell their families about it."

Really? I could hardly believe this. In two months I still hadn't hosted a single person in my home. Now, based on nothing more than a new friend's referral and my own enthusiasm, the US-government-contracted prison was asking if I could help. That should have told me how big the need was.

"When can I start?"

"You'll have to be vetted by Homeland Security," the warden said. He grinned at my shock. "Don't worry, every volunteer has to go through it. But it can take awhile, so just be patient."

Jude was as pleased as I was. "Well, Sarah, what are you waiting for?"

"Nothing," I said, thanking them all. "Just a call from Homeland Security!"

I gulped again. Now it was *really* real.

~

I had a home. I had furniture. I had kitchen cabinets stocked with cans and dry goods. Sadly, I also had time—too much of it. I'd swung open the doors of Casa de Paz in April 2012 with great expectations, but by the end of June, I had hosted exactly one family: Alicia, the mom from Nebraska, and her kids.

Nobody seemed to know about Casa de Paz. But for those who did, the support I got was incredible. Food Bank of the Rockies let me do my shopping there, knowing I was on a limited budget. I had some friendly go-rounds about immigration with a coworker or two at Church Community Builder on Mondays when I drove to Colorado Springs for staff meetings. But those discussions only sharpened my confidence. I appreciated the steadying presence of my boss, Chris. He always emphasized to new employees that my work through Casa de Paz was about people, not politics. And that their dilemmas were real.

Just how real came home heavily to me in July when I got a call from a local woman. Her husband was detained in Aurora ICE.

She wanted her young son and daughter to be able to visit their father, but she didn't have a day off to take them. She'd had to take on several jobs after he was detained. "Do you know anyone who could accompany my children?" she asked me.

"I'll do it!" I knew the insides of Aurora ICE. And I knew what to expect after my visit with the young guy at El Refugio. I would love taking her children to see their daddy.

It turned out I didn't know everything—not even close. The elementary-age daughter and son did fine in the lobby alongside the other families waiting to pass through the metal detector. But the kids clutched my hands tightly as we were led into the narrow, fifty-foot corridor that was the visitation room. On one side was a cinderblock wall; on the other, a row of twelve plexiglass windows. Each window provided a small boothlike space, with a metal stool and an old-style phone, the bulky black kind with a wire-spun cord. Soon, on the other side of the windows, one by one, prison-garbed men filed in and sat down.

A horrible screech startled us all. In a booth nearby, two preschoolers clawed at the plexiglass, crying at the top of their lungs. They were trying to get to their father.

It frightened the little girl and boy clutching me. They looked up for reassurance. "It's okay," I said. "Look, here's your daddy!" Their father sat waving to them in a booth near us, beaming at his kids. I helped the children clamber onto the stool, where they took turns on the phone.

I stood against the opposite wall. There weren't any chairs besides the stools.

A few booths down, a mother tried her best to corral her six-year-old son to talk to his father. The boy shook his head and bounded up and down the narrow room. I stole a glance at the father, who seemed to accept it. The mom snapped her fingers, but the boy ignored her.

Instead, he walked up to adults like me and tapped our hands for attention. He seemed to want to talk to everyone except his absent daddy.

One weary mother was indifferent to her two preschoolers running and shouting as she talked into a phone. Nearby, a little boy held his hands over his ears at the crazy noise echoing through the room.

I couldn't tell whether any of these children understood what was happening. How long had it been since they'd seen their missing daddies? How long since they'd been able to hug or touch them? What had they been told about it all? How did they think about it or talk about it at school?

Standing next to me was a grandmother in an African headwrap and outfit. She held a baby in her arms while toting another in a back-carrier. Her daughter, or perhaps daughter-in-law, sat talking in one of the booths. *At least this family has some extended help,* I thought. The others were single parents struggling alone— all, no doubt, made single by detention. Several people had trouble with their phone lines. A frustrated woman rose and picked up a wall phone to call the guard station to alert someone. Tick by tick, the visitors' one-hour limit was dissipating. I wondered if any were from out of town.

The little girl I'd brought offered me the phone. I whispered a big, "Thank you," and sat down across from her father. With all the positivity I had, I relayed the news his wife had prepped me to tell him.

⌐

"How's it going?" Kim asked. I handed her my rent check.

"There's something I want to do when Christmas comes around," I blurted. "Maybe you've heard of it—Angel Tree? It lets people donate presents to kids with parents in prison."

Kim mused on it. I never asked her for anything. "Sure," she offered, "you could put the tree in the office here. Everybody will see it." Again, she went out on a limb for me, and I was grateful. We both knew even the humblest gift would encourage a visiting child.

Not long after that, I was at the Church Community Builder office when somebody told me I had a visitor. Someone wanted to see me? Standing in the lobby was a guy I didn't know wearing a well-ironed polo shirt and pressed khakis.

"Sarah Elizabeth Jackson?" the guy asked. He seemed friendly but didn't extend a hand. "I'm with the Department of Homeland Security." A measured smile and all business.

It's amazing the sort of command a person like this has. Our receptionist had already set up a room for our interview. I'm sure my coworkers wished they were flies on the wall, even though the guy's battery of questions was fairly routine. I already felt well-prepared from the inch-thick application I'd had to fill out. We even shared a light joke a few times, though he remained at arm's length. *All just a formality,* I thought. Until he asked—

"Do you know anyone in the United States who is here unlawfully?"

I hesitated. *Did not see this coming!* "Um—" I was keenly aware that I knew a lot of undocumented people. The Mexican women whom I used to live with, a guy I'd dated . . . "Um—" I repeated.

Wearing the same measured smile, he rephrased the question: "Has anyone shown you papers that prove they're in the United States unlawfully?"

Wasn't ready for that one either! "Um, no," I answered. "Never."

He looked at his list and moved to the next question.

A month or so later I received an unexpected call. A formal voice from Aurora ICE informed me I was scheduled for a tour of the place. Evidently, I had passed the DHS test; this would be the next step.

The tour I got seemed like the kind given to visiting officials. The female ICE officer showed me the small library area and the infirmary, neither of which had people in it. I wasn't taken to the caged pods. As she led me through the kitchen and laundry areas, I noticed people cleaning them. They wore prison outfits.

"We have a trustee program," the officer explained. "It helps them to earn money while they're here."

I noted that the temperature in the facility was unusually cold. "That's to prevent germs from spreading," the officer said.

Judging by this PR tour, you'd think Aurora ICE wasn't too bad a place to be detained. But that didn't line up with what I knew about the Stewart facility in Georgia and its deaths by suicide. I didn't know what to think.

As I left, she told me I would receive a call once my clearance was final. I thanked her and exited the detention facility—and an unusual sight caught my eye. At the far end of the driveway leading to Aurora ICE, a woman paced along the curb. She was humbly dressed. Her steps were odd: She would take a step, then stop, then look skyward. She was saying something, words I couldn't make out.

The woman was in some kind of distress. I realized she was wailing. I hurried my pace toward her. As I got closer, the sound she made sent a chill through me. She was crying a name: "Miguuuuuuel!"

She wailed out the name again. And wailed. And wailed.

"Senora," I offered, reaching to her. She paid me no attention. "Mama, Mama," I urged reflexively—somehow, I knew this was a mother's wail—"Que pasa, Mama?"

I calmed her enough to tell me in Spanish what was wrong. It was her son, she said—he was inside, and she couldn't see him. I realized she was undocumented and couldn't visit him. All she knew was that her son had been taken from her. The pain she cried was as bad as any in the world.

I'll never forget the sound of it. It pierced me to my bones.

A few days later, Casa de Paz had visitors.

"What is it you do here?" the burly man at my door asked. His voice was good-natured but skeptical. His three teenaged children—who filed into my apartment as he held the door open—had the free-and-easy stride of kids who know the security of a protective father.

All of Alejandro's kids had striking looks. Each was dressed in pressed stylish jeans and shirts. And each wore glasses. The oldest, a son probably approaching twenty, could have passed for a college professor. I saw that the two younger daughters would probably look like professors as well in a few years.

"Hello, welcome, come in," I urged them.

Alejandro had called me an hour earlier. He was checking out of a hotel, ready to return home to Missouri, when his detained wife's lawyer told him about Casa de Paz. If money was an issue, the lawyer said, he should call me. Lodging with me would allow them to stay another day or two. That would mean more time to visit the mom, Julieta, in detention.

I answered Alejandro with my elevator speech. "I don't know all that you're going through," I said, "but this is one thing I can provide." As the kids respectfully seated themselves in the living room, I instructed everyone, "Okay, now tell me about Julieta. I want to know all about your mama, and then we'll have dinner."

First there were a few tears, and then the funny stories began. The kids seemed to ease a bit knowing they would get to see their mom the next day. I could tell from their descriptions that Julieta was a great mom—and utterly distraught being away from them.

As I boiled pasta and they talked, Alejandro rested a palm on the kitchen table. He clearly relished seeing his kids relaxed. Finally, he told me, "I wasn't sure about coming here." He explained why.

Alejandro owned a business in Missouri that had several employees. He and Julieta were pillars in their church. She had never pursued citizenship after they married because it didn't seem like an issue. Then she traveled to Mexico, heartbroken, for her brother's funeral. Her family there was having an especially hard time because her brother had been murdered. When Julieta returned to the US, customs officials arrested her for not having proper documentation.

Terrified and panicked, she was detained in San Diego and later transferred to Aurora. When the kids learned what had happened to their mother, they were crushed. Their family had just absorbed one awful tragedy only to face another.

When Alejandro finished, I kept a respectful silence.

He said, "I've never seen a single person want to help."

"Really?"

"Organizations, maybe," he said, shaking his head, "but not individuals."

The hardest part, he said, was trying to be both mom and dad to his kids. Before the trip, he had tried to curl his youngest daughter's hair but burned it. We both laughed.

The next morning, as the family left for the detention center, each of the kids offered me their gratitude. Then Alejandro gave me a parting word of his own. "This is a gift," he told me.

"Oh, it's my privilege to have you. I hope you can come to see Julieta again soon."

"No," he said, correcting me. "I mean, what you do—it's a gift."

I was puzzled. A simple pasta meal. Makeshift beds in a cramped apartment.

"I've never had an experience like this," he said. "There's an energy here that other places don't have."

The kids chatted outside while their dad stood at the door waiting to muster one last word. "I felt like we were home."

A week later, I got an email from him. He thanked me again for hosting them. "Casa de Paz made me start believing in people," he said.

I couldn't understand why Alejandro and his family—why any of the families I hosted—fell under the intense scrutiny of ICE.

I would be told that it has to do with our nation's recent history—specifically, the attacks of September 11, 2001. But time would show that our country wasn't full of terrorists. Instead, things changed because of what people do with their fears and biases. After 9/11, people began looking at their lifelong neighbors with suspicion, even amazing neighbors like Alejandro and Julieta.

In 2003, a federal policy called Operation Endgame was put into place. Its aim was to deport every person who was in the US without proper documentation. Overnight, nearly 10 million people who had lived and worked here peacefully, many hoping to eventually work toward citizenship like Alejandro and Julieta, were considered a threat to public safety.

That same year, ICE—Immigration and Customs Enforcement—was formed. Before that, our country's immigration system was operated by the INS, the Immigration and Naturalization Service. The INS was known as just that—a service—both to the public and to people migrating here. In 1958, the Supreme Court applauded the agency in 1958 for allowing most migrants to be released while their cases were decided. The formation of ICE would change that completely. The agency that had been revered for its service over seventy years was now commissioned as enforcement. And that began with detention.

Jailing undocumented people is something new in our country. Immigrant detention as we know it didn't exist until the 1980s. It started when thousands of Haitians and Cubans arrived here fleeing harsh political repression. Our government wanted to hold them for legal processing, so it contracted with a private company to build a detention center in Louisiana. That was in 1985. A booming expansion of detention followed. Our government paid huge amounts of money to private companies to build or operate immigrant detention facilities. Corporations formed, the two largest being CoreCivic (previously CCA—Corrections Corporation of America) and the GEO Group.

Immigrant detention was seen as a great investment opportunity. Privately owned detention centers—for-profit immigrant prisons—became about making money. YouTube has videos of corporate executives pitching detention centers as lucrative ventures. Investors descended on it. Today there is a vast network of more than two hundred immigrant detention facilities across the country, and 62 percent of them are for profit.

This all happened in a short period. From 1985 to 1990, the population in immigrant detention grew from 3,000 to 30,000. Last year, the number was 396,448. It's a business that generates $2 billion a year.

That leap didn't happen because more people were coming to the US; they weren't. The unbelievable increase happened for one reason: every private-prison company has powerful lobbyists. The policies formed by their influence directly affect how immigrants in the US are treated. The first thing that happens to them is they're put in jail. Incarceration is the first step in making money for investors.

It's true. Congress passed a national quota that 31,000 to 37,000 undocumented people must be in detention every day. Numbers are higher today; in 2020 ICE held an average of 54,000 per day in its custody. But there's no reason a quota should exist at all. Except for companies to make money.

Every private detention facility has a profit motive. The Aurora ICE Processing Center is one of them, operated by the GEO Group.

When I was given my volunteer tour, I didn't realize that the "trustees" I saw working in the kitchen were being paid one dollar a day. I wasn't told that the facility charges detained people nearly five dollars to make one international phone call. That meant an immigrant with no money had to work a full forty-hour week to talk to a loved one for no more than three minutes.

The more work that detained people do inside a prison at that low wage, the lower the costs of prison maintenance are— and the greater the profits for shareholders.

The financial incentive is clear: put vulnerable people to

work for low wages, then charge them inflated prices for necessities like phone calls.

I pictured Julieta being subjected to all of this.

Studies of private detention facilities show that they operate in far worse conditions than government facilities because of their cost cutting. Immigrants held in private facilities are generally underfed and then charged a fee for simple snacks like chips. They have less access to medical care; on many days, there's not even a medical person on site. The facilities avoid taking sick or elderly people. They employ younger, less-well-trained guards. Their inmate-to-guard ratio is a lot higher. Every bit of this is about saving money. The worse the conditions, the bigger the quarterly checks to shareholders.

Private detention centers also increase their profits with the number of beds they fill in each facility. As beds fill up in one center, detained people get moved like pawns to another facility, sometimes in another state, to fill beds there. People are moved at will, without notice—five thousand people a month. All of that movement is determined either by ICE or by the corporations with no regard to a person's access to their loved ones or lawyers. It becomes a massive burden on the families, costing them terribly in travel expenses and time away from work if they want to visit their loved ones. Families like Alejandro's and Julieta's.

As I learned these things, I wondered: Is there any good reason why a great mom like Julieta should be in a prison system? Why should my Christian sister be held in Colorado rather than in Missouri, near her family and support system? Why should she be coerced to clean a corporation-owned prison for a dollar a day? If she were our mom, our spouse, our church member, wouldn't we protest her incarceration? Wouldn't we go to every length to get her out?

Things weren't this way until immigrant detention became big business. Even ICE leaders saw what was happening.

"Detention is no place for a family," John Sandweg, ICE's former acting director, told a journalist. "It's viewed as the answer to all our immigration problems when it simply is not an effective or efficient tool. And it's not friendly to taxpayers."

It costs $135 a day to hold someone in immigrant detention. That's nearly $3 billion a year. An alternative like electronic ankle bracelets costs only pennies a day and allows a person to work and support their family. Case management is like parole and costs two to seven dollars a day. "Every pilot program I've known about has had a 96 to 99 percent success rate," Sandweg said.

I pictured Julieta as he said, "There's a massive difference between a violent felon or gang member and an individual who came here twenty years ago with their child to find a better life, who never committed a crime, and who now has US citizen children and is deeply integrated into society. You just can't treat them equally."

The US Department of Justice actually concluded that. A few years ago, the DOJ was alarmed at the growth of this for-profit "industry" and considered phasing out all private detention. Congress came to its senses about it all too. It planned to discontinue all private prisons.

Then the 2016 presidential election happened. All that thinking went by the wayside.

In the months that followed, I hosted beautiful families like Alejandro's and Julieta's and saw the indignities they endured, the tears they cried. And I wondered, *Where is their justice, God?*

PART 3

The Journey to One Another

In Louisville, at the corner of Fourth and Walnut, in the center of the shopping district, I was suddenly overwhelmed with the realization that I loved all these people, that they were mine and I theirs, that we could not be alien to one another even though we were total strangers. . . . If only they could all see themselves as they really are. If only we could see each other that way all the time.

—Thomas Merton, *Conjectures of a Guilty Bystander*

CHAPTER 6

The Third Journey

War is what happens to people.

—MARIE COLVIN, JOURNALIST

The lobby at Aurora ICE is as drab and impersonal as any government building gets. Nothing between those walls speaks hope
to anyone who visits. But every once in a while, the long hallway that stretches from that gray room—past the guard station,
toward a set of metal double doors sixty feet away—can be a
path of joy.

That's where your loved one appears as he's released from
detention. The one you've longed to embrace for months or years
steps through those doors, and your heart beats faster. He strides
alongside the guard who escorts him, your grateful smile giving way to tears. Your kids are overcome, too, waiting to bury
their faces in the one they've missed for so long. When he finally
steps through that gate with open arms, your tight, tearful hug
becomes sweeter and sweeter. You don't care about any of the
people shuffling around you in the lobby because all you want is
your embrace to last forever.

If I ever had doubts about what I was doing with Casa de Paz,
the sight of a family reunited erased it all.

Most immigrants who are detained in this country make three journeys. The first is to get here, and it's treacherous and deadly for many. The second is through the US detention system, and that's a perilous trial of its own. The third journey is the one that people take to their final destination, upon their release. For most, it's the hardest journey of all.

Some people are released into jubilation. They're granted asylum or, in rare cases, a special visa. Their final step is out the doors of detention and into the home of a sponsor or a relative or, perhaps, to their own home in the US where they've lived for years or even decades. But for many others in detention, the third journey is one of dread: deportation.

A sweet woman living in the mountains of Colorado drove four hours to stay with me so she could see her husband before he was deported to Mexico.

I was glad to accompany her to Aurora ICE. She and her husband could only press their hands to the glass window, unable to hug or kiss goodbye. Yet the strong, enduring love in their eyes pierced the barrier.

That evening at Casa de Paz, my guest was mostly quiet. When we did talk despite my weak Spanish, she spoke simply, expressing her gratitude, repeating softly, "Gracias. Gracias. Gracias."

I was learning a hard fact about every family who comes to visit someone at Aurora ICE. They never know whether it will be the last time they'll see their loved one. How do they possibly cope?

Sometimes an order of deportation comes with a choice of options—and all are potentially devastating. I hosted a woman whose detained husband was given two options: either leave the country voluntarily and apply for reentry in ten years' time, or risk being deported with no chance to return. The couple decided he would leave voluntarily. "If that's the only way to get him back here," she explained, "it's what we'll do."

Ten years. The thought of it crushed me. I thought of Agustín, the father I met in the border shelter at Agua Prieta. Agustín made a different decision: He couldn't allow his little ones to spend ten years of childhood without their dad. So he kept trying to come back to them.

Another mom I hosted faced a different kind of choice, one that felt cruel. Her husband wasn't a US citizen, but she was, as were their four children. He was about to be deported to Honduras, one of the three most murderous nations in the world. Despite that danger, she considered moving the family there to be with him; she didn't want her children to grow up fatherless. Think about those options: either have your family permanently separated, or risk harm or death for you and your children.

Deportation hangs like an ominous cloud over so many people, suspending them in an agonizing limbo. They are helpless to build a future without the fear of separation or mortal danger. What does that do to their mental state, to their kids? I saw the fearful thoughts swirling in so many families who came to Casa de Paz. They arrived overjoyed to see their loved ones. They left worrying, "What if I never see them again?"

There was no way around that sad possibility. But was there anything that might ease the pain? Something that might bridge their anguished absences from each other?

I struck on an idea: What if I paid regular visits to people in detention after their families left? It wasn't the same as having their loved ones visit, but it was something. I could relay messages from their partners, remind them of their families' support, anything to give them a sense of more regular presence with those they loved. I asked the families if they'd like me to do that.

Everyone said yes. "Oh, he could use a friend. Please, go visit him for us!"

It meant more to those in detention than I expected. For some, I was their only link to the outside world. They never saw trees, grass, sunlight, or sky. Just getting out of their pods was huge, something to break the monotony of the day. Some just needed to vent during the visit; sometimes I did most of the talking. Some just needed a distraction; being alone with their worries was torturous. Every visit was different, but it always ended up being the highlight of the person's week. And mine too. Each time our visit ended, they were already looking forward to the next week.

There was someone to visit almost every day, so I became a fixture in the ICE lobby. The station guards got used to seeing me. After a few weeks, I started to sense a bit of suspicion. One guard had seen me visit five different men on consecutive days. At the week's end, he asked, "Who are you?"

"I live around the corner," I said. "I host families when they come to visit here. Maybe you've seen me with them. Once they leave town, I do their visits for them."

He sized me up as I talked. Finally, he shook his head, convinced. "Casa de Paz—okay. Ha, we all thought you were dating these guys!"

His coworkers had been gossiping! Yet I realized that wasn't a bad thing. *They were noticing.* And now they all knew about Casa de Paz.

Our shared laughter sparked another idea: I should start bringing others with me.

From the outside, maybe it just looked like I had an active social life. The reality is, a tiny community began to form around Casa de Paz. The friends I'd made in advocacy circles had begun dropping by. Word spread further when I started an email newsletter about what I was doing.

Whenever someone showed up, they dove right into

whatever project I was up to: helping sort donated toiletries, stuffing Casa de Paz info cards into cookie bags to hand to lawyers and families exiting Aurora ICE, listening as I talked about my visits inside detention. Everyone was interested. And that encouraged me to tell more people about it. "Hey, Preston," I shouted across the Food Bank, "you're going with me to Aurora ICE next week."

"I am?"

Preston met with José, a Salvadoran man, and we tag-teamed on the staticky phone. In the space of an hour, three people's worlds changed. "His story is so moving," Preston said. "I loved talking with him."

"I'm glad," I said, "because next week you're coming to visit him on your own."

Our visits were treasures to the lonely detained. They told their pod mates there was a place outside that sent people to visit, and soon the pod mates requested visits. The next time I showed up at ICE, the station guard waved me over. "Hey, Sarah," he said, waving a slip of paper. "The warden told me to give this to you. A couple of people are asking for visits."

I stopped in my tracks. I wasn't surprised by the requests, but a guard knew my name? It was the first time anyone at ICE called me by it. I had kind of a moment.

I did know this: People inside needed hope. And, as Anton had said, hope came through visitors. I kept sending them as more and more interested folks showed up at Casa de Paz.

We shared the stories we heard. Together, we were learning about the world's more troubled regions.

I found out why so many internationals make the journey to the US via South America. Ecuador doesn't require a travel visa, so desperate people from every continent fly to its capital, Quito, to start their journey. Asians, Africans, Europeans, and others join together in numbers for safety and take buses, horses, and taxis, sometimes even walking the journey north seeking a life away from the oppression, persecution, crushing poverty, or imminent death that threatened them.

An African man told me about joining an overcrowded boat in Colombia—forty people squeezed into a vessel built for ten—and seeing another boat capsize. They watched everyone drown. "We couldn't get to them on the rapids," he explained.

The people looked out for each other. Townspeople in the countries they traveled through helped them with directions and food. He and others told me that, even in the poorest countries, the detention facilities where they were processed were a hundred times better than in US detention. They were treated with dignity, allowed outside to play soccer, given open buffets to graze from all day long. Once they got to the US, it was a totally different story.

We also learned how ignorant we were of our international neighbors' suffering. And the levels of threat they were running from—threats we couldn't begin to get our heads around.

Hugo, a young Christian from Honduras we visited, was suicidal. He'd been working at his parents' restaurant when a police-backed gang kidnapped his wife and sister, both of whom were pregnant. When the family failed to raise the ransom money, the two women were murdered. Shattered, Hugo went to identify their bodies and described the kidnapping to a couple of policemen there. Eight hours later, Hugo received a call threatening his life. The gang had found out about his report because the police had informed them.

Overnight, Hugo's life became a horror story, the kind we heard more and more about from Central America's northern triangle of Honduras, Guatemala, and El Salvador. Despite the deadly threat, Hugo wasn't persecuted by race, religion, nationality, political opinion, or what's called membership in certain social groups (such as LGBTQ). To claim asylum for him, his lawyer argued his case as political persecution, since the gang was aligned with the police. The court ruled against him—insufficient evidence—and Hugo was deported to Honduras.

We were crushed. Hugo would be hunted the minute he landed. His two closest friends had already been murdered. Now the authorities would know he was coming, and so would the gang. The US court had upheld the letter of the law, but where was justice for an innocent grieving man? Why the decision to send him to a certain death?

The stories we heard weren't easy to take. We sat with people who'd seen their family members slaughtered. They'd been hunted themselves by vicious gangs. Threatened by drug cartels. Chased by fanatical mobs. Hunted by government death squads. When you looked at the sweet people who shared these horrifying stories, they were hard to believe, as hard as when I first listened to Agustín's story at the border two years earlier. And yet by listening, we were sharing their burdens.

Being in the visitation room made me think harder about my role as a protester. I had to ask myself: what was my primary calling, as a voice on the street or as a voice inside Aurora ICE?

I got my answer at a monthly AFSC vigil when my phone lit up. I didn't recognize the number, so I waited for the message.

"I see you protesting," the voice said. It was vaguely familiar. "I want you to know I stand with you. I can't be out there with you because of my employer."

I recognized him—the young assistant warden who wore glasses. The guy who came to Jude's place for a nine-foot burrito!

"But my heart is with you all. I know you've been visiting folks here. I'd like to talk, Sarah. I may have some ideas for you."

He'd been newly married and living on the East Coast when he answered the ad for a junior administrator. The job in Colorado seemed to offer the kind of adventure he and his wife were looking for as they pondered starting a family. He'd sent out a dozen resumes every week with no response except one, and it came within a week. It was from the GEO Group.

He did a bit of research on them, but even so, he never realized he was applying to a prison. He just thought he would be working with international people awaiting official entry into the US. The part he looked forward to was learning other people's cultures. The detention part became clear to him only during the phone interview. Still, he and his wife were up for it, and he accepted GEO's offer.

Immediately, he was shocked by two things: first, the prison-like atmosphere, with people locked in. He thought detention centers were just what the name implied: places to detain people until their cases are heard. This place? It was punitive. Yet the people hadn't committed a crime.

Then there were the power-hungry coworkers. They lorded their positions over the detained people in disturbing ways. Every day he saw at least one person being abused or mistreated. The breakdown was fifty-fifty between workers who were kind and those who were abusive. If one of the latter was having a bad day, they took it out on the detained people.

"Could you change the TV channel?"

Couldn't be bothered.

"The slippers you gave me are torn. They're making my feet ache. Can I get another pair?"

No response.

There was retribution against those who filed complaints. A Russian man had been detained for four-and-a-half years—in ten different facilities around the country. The assistant would learn that that kind of constant movement was a form of punishment.

The only place a detained person could turn for help was their immigration lawyer. But only one in ten people had one because so few could afford it. Thankfully, an awesome non-profit group came in weekly to tell people about their legal rights.

RMIAN—the Rocky Mountain Immigrant Advocacy Network—referred them to pro bono lawyers who might be able to take their cases. They also did mental health evaluations to see if people qualified for help that way.

The warden's assistant was thankful for this. He also drew solace from having a boss like the warden, someone with compassion and, better yet, backbone. Both traits were needed for the sakes of the detained people. Yet company policy dictated certain things, like people being wakened at 5:00 a.m. for breakfast. Lunch was at 10:30 a.m. Dinner came at 4:00, and then no food was available till the next day. People weren't allowed to save any part of their meal to satiate the hunger of the next thirteen hours. The guards did occasional "dorm shakes" to find any food that might be hidden away.

Beans were served at almost every meal. Sometimes they were the main course. Some meals were no more than gruel. Each meal's price point was capped at one dollar or less—GEO was a private company, after all, so shareholder profits took precedence over basic nutrition. The meals were delivered to the pods, and the smell that filled the living area was terrible—like a big vat of grease. A pregnant guard always avoided the pods at mealtime to avoid getting nauseated.

Medical staff were onsite only part of the time. On weekends, the infirmary was closed altogether. Eyewear wasn't considered a medical necessity. If people's glasses got broken, they weren't repaired—not even with masking tape. People's main recreation was either reading or watching TV, but without their glasses, headaches were common.

The entire facility was continually understaffed. People worked twelve-hour days over and over, burning out. The warden hit a brick wall every time he requested another hire. The assistant regretted not joining the union; he would never make that mistake again. He and the warden had so little to work with that they constantly looked for help through outside resources, relying on people like my friend Jude Del Hierro.

So why did he stay on? The assistant told himself he could bring people some joy and smiles, some happy distraction from their daily misery. Helping people was his calling; it was the reason he entered this career path. But a compassionate person here could go only so far to improve the lives of detained people. It would risk his job.

He did go above and beyond for people several times. Somebody told him about a woman in detention, a super-educated Latinx whose baby was being cared for by relatives in Denver. This new mom was lactating and wanted to express milk for her baby. She went to the infirmary to see if a hand pump was available. She was denied all help. Instead, the staff person handed her two ibuprofen tablets and an ace bandage, saying, "Wrap this tightly around yourself. It'll dry up your milk." She was astounded. She ended up self-expressing in a bathroom. The assistant heard about it and made sure the milk got to her baby. It angered him to think how easily an alternative could have helped that mom and her baby. His own wife was pregnant with their first child at the time.

He resisted despair as he saw people's spirits continually broken. Week after week, whenever someone was inducted into the facility, no matter how upbeat their personality, they got depressed in a matter of weeks. He could read their thoughts: "What's my kid doing right now? How is my wife able to pay our bills?"

ICE's policies on phone calls and contact made it hard for them to be in touch with loved ones. Sometimes their families didn't even know where they were. Often when people are detained, their families have no way to locate them. They could be arrested and transported anywhere. A concerned young law student in California saw this happen to a classmate's family. The classmate spent weeks trying to locate her mother and father, who were being detained in different states. And the parents had no way to reach their daughter because when they were detained, they didn't have money on hand to call from detention. It was a dilemma of access. For Christina Fialho, the alarmed law student, this was a violation of basic rights. As she learned more about the US detention system, Christina began a movement to have hotlines installed inside detention facilities. She also located a few fledgling visitation programs around the country—there were only a handful at the time—so that a person being detained could know their voice was heard outside the facility. One of those dozen visitation programs Christina called was Casa de Paz. She and I became fast friends.

Around that time, the warden's assistant was pained over the treatment of a vibrant young Bangladeshi. This young man was intense in all the right ways—fiery and funny, a natural leader. He had escaped persecution from a radical Muslim faction. The assistant saw that his strength of spirit had potential to help lead others, so he recommended him to the program director.

The young Bangladeshi was given a training role inside the pods and he dove into the job. Yet despite the daily progress and small victories he brought to people, abuse from guards and the oppressive environment wore on him. As weeks passed, his spirit sank. All his positive energy dissipated. He grew combative. At one point, he was accused of taking candy bars from the kitchen. Within a couple of months, the bright young man had shut down completely.

And then something happened.

In small pockets of the facility, the assistant saw a few people's spirits lifted. Depressed men began smiling again. Those men brought encouragement to others in their pod. Little by little, morale lifted above the despair. It even affected some of the guards. Their work passed better on certain days.

These were only small changes in a big place, but any positive difference in that kind of environment was noticeable. The assistant saw it was because of our visits. "Could we get more?" he asked.

Morale rose among Casa de Paz volunteers too as word spread through our little community. What a gift it was to know the people we visited. Even longtime advocates in the community saw what could happen to supply hope inside Aurora ICE. One by one, people in our orbit stepped up to join what I called our "visitation program." I was more than happy to send more volunteers their way.

"I know somebody in particular who could use a visit," the assistant said. "He's having a lot of suicidal thoughts." It was the young Bangladeshi man. I contacted two women who'd been interested in visitation. Working in tandem, they could visit him as often as possible. Beneath his depression, the women could see what a bright light shone from within the guy. After their first visit, one of them told me, "I would be friends with him anyway if we met outside of all this." They went on to help him find legal aid. Eventually, after a long series of retributive actions against him, he won asylum.

For the first time in a couple of years, I returned to a great pleasure: coordinating people and encouraging them forward, just like I'd done as a church administrator and an amateur volleyball coach. That led to invitations to speak. Volunteers invited me to their churches, and I recruited more people to have their lives changed by knowing friends in detention.

My talk at a United Church of Christ touched a grandparent couple, Ted and Lisa Lytle. When it came to immigration, Ted felt overwhelmed. On the one hand, there was border security to consider, but as a Christian it pained him that people of other nationalities and faiths were being demonized in the media. He felt helpless about it all until he heard me describe Casa's work. When he and Lisa offered to volunteer, I paired them to visit a Muslim man from Pakistan.

Abbas has presence, to say the least. As the Lytles settled in front of the plexiglass, they were struck by the Pakistani man's combination of dignity and gentleness. He was an upstanding Muslim, and he wanted to assure the Lytles, "There is nothing in the Koran to perpetrate violence on anyone. It is about love." That interpretation of Islam led to Abbas's persecution. He wanted an education for his daughters, which isn't allowed in the culture. He had owned a retail store in the same valley as Malala Yousafzai, the young girl who defied the Taliban and won the Nobel Peace Prize. The Taliban burned Abbas's business to the ground.

He led his family to safety in a refugee camp in Peshawar. Then, purely on faith, Abbas left for the United States to seek asylum. His confidence in the fairness of US law didn't waver. When the Lytles visited him at Aurora ICE, he had been detained for twenty-two months.

"How are you holding up?" Lisa asked.

Abbas smiled. "I understand law and order," he said of detention. "My country is very corrupt. I am not happy inside here, but I appreciate the legal process."

His confidence in that process was tested. ICE agents coerced and bullied Abbas to sign a form to be deported. Abbas refused. They taunted him that by appealing he had already been denied asylum, that he was wasting time away from his family. Abbas sat firm. He believed in the law.

Two weeks later, I called the Lytles with great news: Abbas was at the Casa. "He won his case! Can you come over?"

They all hugged, wept, and talked for three hours.

"What about those twenty-two months?" a smiling Ted asked Abbas.

"It feels like twenty-two minutes now," Abbas reflected. His faith in the law was rewarded.

Abbas got a job in Denver and worked to bring his family to the US. He visited the Lytles as if they were family, and after one evening-long catch-up session, the couple convinced him to stay overnight with them. Ted stayed up to email me that a prayer had been profoundly answered.

"A year ago, I was deflated about the state of the world. Nothing made sense, and I couldn't do anything about it. Tonight, I have a Muslim man from Pakistan sleeping in my house. He has escaped harm. He's going to bring his family here. And he feels like a brother to me in a way I can't explain. Thank you, Sarah, for Casa de Paz."

A volunteer named Nancy, a career Peace Corps worker, alerted me to a struggling man she was visiting in detention. Ricardo was from Mexico and a devout Catholic who only wanted to find work to support his family. He ended up unwittingly trafficked and forced into serving a drug cartel. He had told his story to everyone in detention—pod mates, lawyers, even guards—and everyone advised him to self-deport. At least that would save him from the downward spiral detention was causing him.

Ricardo was indeed breaking down, but it was because no one would believe him. As Nancy sought legal help for him, I decided to send him an additional visitor. I had only recently met Daniel Ponce de Leon, a student at Denver Seminary, which is well-known for its evangelical theology. Daniel had earned a law degree in Veracruz, Mexico, and was preparing for ministry. An earnest, focused guy with a sense of humor to balance his forthright convictions, Daniel was skeptical about my work at first. He didn't get why a young woman was taking in strangers to her tiny apartment in a rough part of town.

Then he visited Ricardo in Aurora ICE. This guy's story—of cartels, kidnapping, and torture—sounded like a movie. But Daniel sensed it was the real deal.

Yet that wasn't what struck Daniel most. As he searched Ricardo's eyes, a troubling thought kept churning in him: "That could be me." The plexiglass separating him from Ricardo was a mirror into Daniel: In it, he saw a Mexican and Christian caught up in horrific circumstances just by trying to love his family as best he could. A good man tortured by a cartel, subjected to government detainment, burdened by an exacting judicial system, and heavily doubted by government lawyers. What was happening to Ricardo, his brother in Christ, could happen to him.

Daniel felt the weight of it. Watching Ricardo, he wondered, "How does he have such hope?" The guy's belief was contagious. He was breaking, it was clear to see, but his faith was real. His hopeful attitude reached into Daniel and touched something. What, exactly?

Daniel recognized it as the life of God stirring in a struggling human heart. Where there should have been no hope by any measurement, hope sprang up.

Their visit came at a pivotal time for Daniel. He knew that in seminary, real-life issues can get compartmentalized into abstract talk. Ricardo was no abstraction. Meeting him showed Daniel clearly how the world's most vulnerable are treated unjustly, and why Jesus taught so much on justice for them. That had not been part of Daniel's evangelical formation; it had focused mostly on personal salvation. He would read the Bible differently now—more deeply and thoroughly, not ignoring one subject in Scripture to emphasize another. He started to see the whole gospel that Jesus preached—that it focused just as much on justice, on loving the vulnerable, as it did on salvation.

The encounter affected how Daniel saw Casa de Paz too. If undocumented Mexican nationals living in Denver's shadows could receive this kind of support—deep Christian love—they would feel valued, seen, not forgotten. That was Jesus' gospel.

"I think I understand better what you're about," Daniel told me after his visit with Ricardo. "I'd like to know more."

With awe-inspiring aid from Colorado Legal Services, Ricardo received a T visa, granted to immigrants who've been trafficked. It allowed him to stay in the United States.

What Ricardo did with his freedom is amazing. As soon as he received his state identification card, he went back to Aurora ICE and visited everyone he knew in detention. He had something in abundance that he wanted them to have too: hope.

As Nancy says, "People in detention need someone to walk alongside them—hearing their story, helping them get what the law entitles them to, and watching them thrive. In the end, they'll sacrifice to give that help back to others who need it."

And yet nobody might ever have heard him. It happened because of a simple visitation program. Even the smallest act—like listening—can change everything.

CHAPTER 7

To Sleep with a Thousand Strangers

You yourselves are our letter, written on our hearts, known and read by everyone. You show that you are a letter from Christ, the result of our ministry, written not with ink but with the Spirit of the living God, not on tablets of stone but on tablets of human hearts.

—2 CORINTHIANS 3:2–3

Imagine you're from Kinshasa. Or Islamabad. Or Kuala Lumpur. Home is where you ran from, to escape being killed. You dream about it on many nights. Maybe you're dreaming about it when you're awakened by the guard. A different guard from the one who shut out the lights a few hours earlier. When you rouse, it must be around midnight. And you remember you're in this cage.

The guard tells you you've been released. *Why? Have I been paroled?* Maybe for some other reason you don't understand. All you know is that now, as you stand in the dimly lit lobby of this prison, you're handed a large envelope. The station guard fixes you in his gaze and says, "You have to leave." You don't know what he means. Expressionless, he nods toward the exit.

Clutching the envelope, you step through the doors and into night. It's a strange darkness, a world nothing like your own.

Your senses awaken violently. They've been shut down for months by the sealed existence you've lived. You're immediately disoriented. The sidewalks look different from any you've known. The roads look different. You don't know where anything leads. Even the trees look different. Everything around you looks different except the black sky. You don't know north from south, east from west. You don't know what city you're in. Much less that you're in a certain state with a name. Or that it's thousands of miles from wherever you entered the country.

You have no place to go. You don't know anyone. You have no money. No way to communicate because you don't know this foreign language. All you have is the envelope, a sheaf of process papers given to you by a judge. It may tell you to show up in court four months from now for your hearing. Maybe it says where to show up. But you're not sure how you'll manage any of that. Or where you'll stay in the meantime. If you miss that court date, the judge won't assume the best about you. You'll probably lose your case; he'll think you skipped out, and you'll be deported. Back to the country you came from, even though you fled it to save your life.

You're not allowed to work or make money until your work permit arrives, and that could take months. To work otherwise is breaking the law, and it disqualifies you from being here. How will you get by? Where will you go to live?

You hear the faint sound of traffic. Possibly a major road nearby. Maybe someone there can help. There it is, you see it a few blocks away. Those are buses you see driving past. And now a train bell. So you begin walking until, yes, you see a bus stop. It's across the railroad tracks. You can ask someone there where to go. They'll know where to steer you.

You stand at the bus stop for a long while, and finally a bus arrives. The door opens, but you don't know how to speak to the driver. He keeps saying something to you, but you don't know what it is. You can only take a tentative step up. He shakes his head and talks louder to you. He is impatient. Finally, he waves you back, shuts the door, and drives off.

You stand there not knowing what to do. It is the middle of winter. You entered the border of the US in summer, wearing a short-sleeved shirt and loose pants. So that's all you're wearing now—the clothes that were handed back to you as you were released. No coat, no sweater, no boots or hat. The temperature is dropping.

A car drives up. The window rolls down, and a man leans his head out. He smiles at you and holds up a bag of something. Drugs. He points down the street to a man standing near a gas station down the block. The man in the car shakes the bag. In his other hand, he holds up US money. His offer becomes clear: he'll give you the money if you deliver the bag to the man down the street.

You're desperate. If you'd had that US money, the bus driver would have accepted you. But you can't do what this man is asking. You shake your head no.

Another car drives up. A different man leans his head out the window. He beckons you over. He holds up a bus ticket. As you approach him to try to communicate, you realize he wants you to perform a sexual act.

What is this place? you think. Inside, you cry out to God.

That moment—when a person in detention is released—may be the worst gap in the entire US immigration system. It's a crucial moment in a person's life. And for our society.

If you're a Christian, and you remember Jesus' parable of the good Samaritan, this is the scene where you come across the traveler who's been left lying by the side of the road. The one who's in desperate need but is bypassed by everyone.

That's why I picked up the phone when ICE called.

"I'm an officer at the detention center," the voice said. "We have a young woman here who's about to be released. She has on a T-shirt and jeans—it's all she's got."

I glanced out the window at the swirling January blizzard.

"There's no one to pick her up, and no place for her to go," the guard said. "Would you be willing to come get her?"

My heart raced. "Sure," I said, as calmly as I could manage. Awkwardly, I thanked him for the call and hung up. Wait, what just happened? ICE called *me?*

The warden had probably told him to phone me. I was glad for that. Still, my palms were sweating.

I was about to host my first guest from immigrant prison.

When I entered the lobby, she sat under the fluorescent lighting in one of the molded-plastic chairs. She had a trash bag on her lap—that's what ICE gives people who are being released to carry their belongings. Her dark hair and skin contrasted with the sterile industrial-white walls.

She said her name was Flor. Spanish for flower.

"Would you like to come to my home, Flor? I have a coat for you there." Oh, my, why didn't I bring a coat for her? Too nervous! I offered her mine, but she shook her head.

Outside in the swirling storm, Flor didn't flinch. She walked calmly as if there weren't a wild storm tossing flakes through the air like an outdoor blender.

"Where are you from?" I asked.

"De Guatemala," she said.

I had learned from Anton Flores-Maisonet what life was like in Guatemala. It was one of the world's five most murderous nations. The police there don't pursue 95 percent of the crimes. That's because they're in league with the gangs that commit the crimes. Life was dangerous for anyone like Flor. Here, now, I thought about what might have happened if Flor been released alone into the blizzard. She wouldn't even know which way to turn on the sidewalk. And that wouldn't matter, because she wouldn't have anyplace to go. And no way to get to her distant relatives in Utah.

Not just a serious gap in our immigration system. A deadly gap.

I thanked God again for the guard's phone call.

Calls started coming more frequently from the station desk at Aurora ICE. And I was grateful.

After one call, I strode over to pick up a man who sat in the lobby in pajamas. That's what he was wearing when ICE arrested him in the middle of the night. He was handcuffed and removed from his home as his kids watched in terror. Back at the Casa, I offered him a look at the few men's clothes donated by people who'd dropped by. A humble, gracious man, he tried some on. He didn't care that they weren't a perfect fit.

"The best thing about being out of detention," he told me over a mouthful of chili, "is that I feel like a human being again." I took a photo of him the next morning as he knelt for his preschool-age daughter to race into his arms. It was hard to believe: One day, he was considered an animal in a cage and a danger to society and treated as subhuman. The next, he was released as the gentle, tender father his children loved. How did that add up?

The guard station called at all times of day, and I always answered. One came after midnight. "There's a jail south of Denver, in Dove Valley," the guard said. "It contracts with ICE to hold people. They're releasing a guy tonight and he's got nowhere to go. Can you take him?"

"Of course I can! Thanks for letting me know."

Dove Valley? What's that? I had no idea where this place was.

I decided to call Daniel Ponce de Leon. He volunteered at Casa regularly, and—well, what was one late phone call to a dedicated volunteer?

"Are you crazy?" he said. "What on earth are you doing? You're picking up a guy from jail?"

"You know I can't turn down these calls when I get them," I said. "If I do, they may never call me again." Honestly, I still needed to work on my boundaries a bit.

"You can figure that out some other time. But tonight, you can't do this thing."

"Okay, I'll figure all that out. But—will you go?"

He did. And we argued the whole way.

The guy we picked up was just like any other guest, of course. Grateful to be free. Grateful to have a place to go. And Daniel's challenge was why I appreciated his friendship. He asked questions that others wouldn't because my boldness could be pretty persuasive.

My ex-boyfriend, Jorge, was concerned for me too. When he found out I was hosting men, he got protective. He offered to put me up at his place whenever men stayed at Casa de Paz.

All of this brought up the obvious question among friends and volunteers: Wasn't I afraid? Single men, released from immigrant prison—and me alone with them?

Of course fear was a factor, I answered. But not mine. *Theirs.*

I was completely serious about this, and still am. These men had just been released from a long, terrible jail term. They weren't likely to do anything that risked sending them back there or getting them deported. And there was another, more urgent issue for them: Why should they trust *me*?

At no time since they left their home country had they been able to trust anyone. Their own government abused them. Their "coyotes" abandoned them. Paid handlers misled or betrayed them. They could be trafficked. There was no help at ICE about the awful conditions inside. Now, as they're released, a guard in the lobby tells them to wait around for someone who wants to come and pick them up. Why would they possibly trust some unknown person who wanted to do that?

It didn't surprise me why some guests were reluctant to come to Casa de Paz. *Why is this lady being so nice? What does she want? Where does she want to take me, and why? Will she ask my family for money before I'm allowed to leave her home?* They simply shook their heads no.

Those who did come with me were often nervous. So anxious that they had no appetite. That said a lot, because most were starving when they got out of ICE.

Some were tentative about everything. I would open the fridge door, wave an inviting hand to them, and they would stand expressionless. Nothing. If they needed a coat or some clothing item, I would open the closet with a gesture, "Take something." No movement, nothing.

I would show them the apartment, and tell them in earnest, "Mi casa es su casa." But they went straight to the bedroom, shut the door, and didn't come out. I'm sure many times they didn't sleep at all, unsure of what the night would bring in this strange place. They didn't emerge until their families or friends arrived for them. Or until I drove them to the bus station.

It broke my heart the first time I reassured a guest, "Let's get you home," and he flinched. Home was the country he was fearful of. After that, I made sure to start saying, "Let's get you where you need to go."

I also learned to say as I opened the door for them, "Welcome to Casa de Paz. Bienvenidos, bienvenue," and point them to the coffee table where a bottle of water and a simple snack from the

Food Bank awaited them. Sometimes it helped when I found a channel on YouTube to play music from their home country.

It thrilled me to see a guest napping on the sofa. It told me they felt safe, comfortable enough to rest openly, as if they were home. Those moments reminded me of the peaceful scenes I'd witnessed at El Refugio, peace enveloping people in their unself-conscious moments, signaling that they felt secure: Kids playing quietly on the floor. A mom able to enjoy a simple cup of tea. Images of traumatized people finally at rest.

Here at Casa de Paz, I saw yet another kind of peace. It was the peace of a traveling stranger who'd been beaten, left for dead on the side of the road, and brought to an inn where their wounds could be tended and start to heal. That's a spearate kind of peace—a survivor's peace.

I remember the first time a guest asked me, "Why are you doing this?" His first language was French, which I didn't know, but his second language was Spanish, which was my second language too.

We struggled to communicate, and I had trouble finding the words to describe my faith to him. "Porque . . . porque . . ." I stammered, and finally landed on something I knew to be true: "Porque usted es mi familia." *You're my family.*

That seemed about right. He nodded, smiling.

I decided then it was more important that people in our care experience the love of God instead of hearing any words *about* God. I fell back on the old saying I'd learned as a homeschooler, something ascribed to Francis of Assisi: "Speak the gospel, and when necessary, use words."

People we visited in detention began asking Casa volunteers the same question: "Why are you doing this?" The volunteers came to me to know how to answer.

"Whatever your reason for doing this, tell them," I suggested. "I don't think any reason would be a bad one."

At a previous time in my life, I would have taken my house guest's question as a "witnessing opportunity" to explain the Christian gospel. Looking back, I think my Spanish limitations with him were a gift. Just as some people have reasons to flinch over the word *home,* others have reasons to flinch over any mention of religion. Especially when they've fled a religion that wants to kill them.

One guest grew up in a Muslim country, and each day on his way to the mosque, he passed a Methodist church. The people there were always friendly to him, their waves and brief chats with him full of warmth, and he was intrigued. He began researching Christianity. The more Ibrahim read, the more he was convinced about their Jesus, and he decided to devote his life to him.

Ibrahim's community was not happy about it. A group of men confronted him, but he told them he wouldn't retract his conversion because it was real. Enraged, they mobbed Ibrahim and beat him, leaving him for dead. A man passing by saw that he was still breathing. "Is there somewhere I can take you?" he asked.

"To the church."

As Ibrahim recovered, word got back to him: "If they see you, they will kill you." And so he fled the country.

Over dinner at Casa de Paz, Ibrahim showed me the printed death threat, a version of a bounty poster. He had used it to win his asylum case. It was chilling to see. I can't imagine what he felt when he first read it.

"I'm a Christian," Ibrahim summarized his story for me. "If that means I have to die for Jesus, I won't go back on it."

Yet as strong as his faith was, Ibrahim's journey here had been full of abuse. It cast doubts for him over the kindness of strangers. When he first walked into the Casa alongside the friend who'd picked him up, Ibrahim turned from wall to wall, taking in the warm setting. "Is this even real?" he asked. "Am I dreaming?"

I pinched his arm and smiled. "You're not dreaming. It's real."

With so many hurting guests, stories like Ibrahim's encouraged me. I wasn't bothered at all that some guests didn't stay in touch after they left. I understood why: once their traumatic detention was behind them, they didn't want to be reminded of any part of it.

Yet it was different for a lot of others. People who'd suffered the worst traumas somehow summoned the strength to glance backward so they could pass on the peace they'd received. Their gestures signaled a compassionate conviction: *Never forget those in need behind you.*

I once drove a humble woman from Guatemala to the bus station. As she got out, she handed me a crumpled bill. It was her last ten dollars. I knew this, because she showed me her few possessions when she arrived at Casa de Paz. "No, no, I can't accept this," I told her. Then I realized she wasn't giving it to me. She meant it for those who came after her.

I remember a certain African man who came to the Casa. "Do you have an iron?" he asked me first thing. "Yes, I'll get you an iron," I said curiously. He explained that he wanted his outfit to be pressed when he reunited with his family.

"And do you have a piece of paper?"

I handed him a notebook, along with a pen. He wrote down a name and gave it to me. "This is my friend," he said. "He is locked up. Is it possible for someone to visit him?"

It was clear to me these folks loved their neighbor *as themselves.* They might not have been aware they were doing exactly what Jesus preached: "In everything, *do to others what you would have them do to you,* for this sums up the Law and the Prophets" (Matt. 7:12, my emphasis).

I would never know what Casa guests felt. But I was beginning to feel something alongside them. A lot of advocates use the word *solidarity* to describe their relationship to the people they walk beside. Maybe I was beginning to know what that meant—not just the idea of it but the sense, the smell, the taste of it. Still, to me, the term pales next to what deep down I understand these actions to be: love.

To sleep with a thousand strangers? Strangers like these amazing people? It was no scandal. I was just an immigrant for a night, alongside them. And humbled to be in their godly company.

CHAPTER 8

He Had Compassion

It is not up to me who I am supposed to love.

—Lauren Daigle, singer/songwriter

In April 2012, a highly respected Mennonite couple was hosting heady theological forums in Mexico City. Rebeca Gonzalez Torres and Fernando Perez were well-known for leading ideological discussions of the highest caliber. At one point, it was decided their two bright minds belonged in the US, where they could start a Spanish-speaking congregation. One of their scouting trips would be in Denver. That's when I heard from Vern Rempel, the Mennonite pastor who gave me rent money to start Casa de Paz.

"Sarah, there's a couple here from Mexico who are looking to start a church," Vern said. "Really sharp people. Do you think—"

"They can stay at the Casa!" I blurted. "Tell them they can help me."

Within a week, an affable man with a warm laugh and an acutely observant woman—a couple in their forties—sat facing me on my hand-me-down sofa. Their English wasn't strong, nor was my Spanish, but their nods were gracious as we tried to comprehend each other. They kept looking over my shoulder at the apartment, probably wondering how three people would live here. Then I told them there would be other guests: people released from detention, as well as visiting families.

They looked worried.

"Don't fret, I'll stay with Jorge," I assured them. "Es mi amigo. Mi casa es tu casa ahora!"

Jorge, my ex-boyfriend, was still the most honorable man I knew then. A hardworking carpet layer who rose every day at 5:00 to start his job. Friends had urged him to apply for DACA, the temporary protected-status program for immigrants brought to the US as children by their parents. Jorge was too old by a week to qualify. But because he had no birth certificate, his friends urged him to fudge his age. It was only a week! He refused.

My moving in with Jorge tells you how unorthodox my situation was. I was a full-time outreach leader with a growing circle of supporters in my work, yet I was still forced to sofa-surf with an ex.

"What exactly do you do here?" Rebeca asked.

"Oh, it's a lot," I began: Visit people in detention. Pick them up when they're released. Call their loved ones. Help them arrange travel. Host families who visit. Cook with them. Help take kiddos to visit their mom or dad in detention.

It was a lot for anyone to take in, much less non-native-English speakers. I kept forgetting how bizarre the immigrant detention system must have sounded. Rebeca drew a legal pad from her handbag. "Do you have a pen I can borrow?"

"Yes! A lady brought pens just yesterday. She came exactly when I'd run out of pens, can you believe it? I was using high-lighters to write things down, and then she just showed up out of the blue."

"How many people have you 'hosted' so far?" Fernando asked.

"Oh, about fifty. No, forty. No, sixty. I think."

"How do you get all this done?" Rebeca asked.

"Oh, people come by. There's Rhoda, maybe you know her? And Debbie? They're Mennos too. And a guy named Daniel, from Denver Sem—"

It must have sounded so disordered. But it was all crystal clear in the logistics of my head.

"And your mission, Sarah," Rebeca asked, "can you describe it?"

My mission? "To help immigrants!"

"To help immigrants," Rebeca mused. "A big concept. And very broad."

Fernando was on his feet, looking around. "Sarah, what is all this?" he asked, peeking in the coat closet.

"Those are donations. People drop them off all the time."

"Lingerie?" Fernando asked. Rebeca craned a glance.

I suddenly remembered a male guest from Africa who needed a jacket for cold weather. He'd picked out a woman's coat. I tried to explain to him that it was a female item and might not fit him properly, but he wasn't fazed. He couldn't be dissuaded.

"And this?" Fernando pointed to a stack of boxes in a corner. One thousand rolls of dental floss. All donated. A dog bed. Some towels with holes and stains on them.

"Some people are giving what they don't need," Rebeca observed.

Fernando poked his head around the corner to inspect the bathroom. He chuckled. "May we ask a volunteer to bring a shower curtain?"

We all laughed. And Rebeca kept taking notes.

They were great hosts. If a guest needed a shirt or a blouse and the closet didn't produce one, Fernando and Rebeca donated their own. I absolutely loved that. I handed Rebeca what money

I could so she could go to Ross to buy bras and sanitary items for our female guests.

Up till then, I'd given my Casa guests pretty much run of the house. But Rebeca wrote down some house rules to maintain a bit of order. She also got me thinking about a mission statement. And a values statement. I hadn't thought about those things since the early days of Church Community Builder. I loved it. Something dormant came alive in me.

I took Rebeca and Fernando with me to Aurora ICE to do visitation. They were surprised that so many people they met were African. They assumed everyone inside would be Latin American. "Indian, Haitian, Chinese," Fernando remarked. "I had no idea." French was the couple's second language, so between that, their broken English, and their native Spanish, they could communicate with most people they visited.

I taught them how to do pickups in the ICE lobby. One of the first guests they brought to Casa de Paz was a Chinese guy. Communication was reduced to nods and gestures. The guy wanted to smoke, so Fernando gestured for him to go outside on the balcony. The guy thought he was being kicked out! Pretty soon Fernando discovered Google Translate, the app that interfaces every language with another. A simple app like that became a miracle worker for us.

Then they brought home Babar, a man from Africa who spoke French. "Something to eat?" Rebeca asked.

"I would like to talk to my family," Babar said softly. "They think I am dead."

"Dead?"

"It has been three years," he said. "They don't know what happened to me." Babar had spent more than two years making his way to the US, then another eight months in detention.

Rebeca set up a video chat for Babar with his family. As the screen image came up, connecting Colorado to Africa, Babar descended into tears. Everyone on-screen shrieked, "Babar! Babar! Look, our dad is alive! Look at me, Dad!"

Rebeca and Fernando were reduced to a puddle.

For some reason, more women than usual were being released from ICE. "Would you like to use the phone?" Rebeca or Fernando would offer. "Take a shower? Are you hungry?" More than one woman answered, "I have a craving for a certain food. I haven't had it for a long time."

"What is it? We'd love to make it for you."

"No, please—I'd like to make it. Is that okay?"

"Of course," the couple said, pointing to the kitchen. "Whatever you need."

The women relaxed as they prepared the food. As they shared the dish with their hosts, they talked as if an inner door had swung open, and they reminisced. Smell is the sense most closely associated with memory, and the aromas of food served up palpable thoughts of their families. They talked about their children, their partners, their parents, their hometowns, the paths they strolled. These women had entered Casa de Paz shyly. As they ate, they spoke as if they were home.

This is therapy, Rebeca and Fernando noted.

Several of the women insisted on preparing a meal for the next guests. "There are tamales in the freezer," they would tell Rebeca or Fernando. It wasn't a gesture of convenience. They wanted the guests who followed them to have the same joy.

They also wanted to *walk* as well as *talk*. A block away from the apartment is a park, and Fernando accompanied them there for their safety. Those walks led to deeper talks. The women often cried. They spoke with great feeling, emotions that had lain dormant for months or years in detention. Even if it rained, they insisted on walking. That too was therapy.

Fernando marveled over this to Rebeca and me. "When they talk, it's like a new expression for them," he said. "A feeling of life for these women. They've been through such pain, such grief."

"Logotherapy," Rebeca noted. *Healing.*

"One of my favorite moments," I told them, "is when I simply say, 'Welcome.' You know they haven't heard that word in a long time."

"And language is no barrier," Fernando added. "Even without this"—he pointed to Google Translate on his phone—"there is no obstacle to connecting. The limitation is only here," he said, pointing to his head.

"This is such a gift," Rebeca reflected. "To meet them, to hear their stories. Sarah, do you know what you have?"

Fernando shook his head. "People aren't percentages," he said. He was reflecting on the couple's professional reality before coming to Casa de Paz. Everything for them had been theoretical, ideological. "'He had compassion on them,'" Fernando reflected. He was quoting Matthew 9:36, the passage where crowds sat before Jesus, desperate for hope.

One of the most desperate guests was Gloria. After being released from ICE, Gloria was shattered. She was a twenty-six-year-old transgender person from Mexico. Her home culture despised transgender people. That's putting it mildly. LGBTQ migrants are ninety-seven times more likely to be sexually assaulted than others in detention.

Before her release, Gloria was locked in solitary for six months. That's where ICE often placed trans people, if not in the medical unit. In solitary, Gloria had access to one hour of TV a day. Beyond that, she had no interaction—just her own thoughts, month after month. The isolation got to her. She worried what her fate would be, whether she would be deported back to danger. She began to pray, "God, if you exist . . ."

Gloria won asylum, and Fernando and Rebeca brought her to the Casa. She was the first transgender person they had ever met. At first, it was difficult and strange for them. They weren't sure how to relate to her.

Gloria mostly sat on the couch, disconsolate. She would talk and then fall silent. Her deep pain came out in spurts of words and tears. All day and into the night, she talked and cried. Rebeca and Fernando simply sat with her.

For three days, Gloria detailed to them her loneliness in the world. She especially confided in Rebeca, speaking heart to heart. They spoke over meals, and Fernando accompanied Gloria on walks. The couple basically shared Gloria's pain for three days, helping to bear her heavy story. And Fernando and Rebeca saw her heart.

One day Gloria couldn't stop crying. Fernando rose and embraced her like a daughter. "You're free," he told her. "You are family."

She wept with different tears now. Wiping her face, she whispered, "I want to cook for you."

Gloria's lawyer had said she needed just three days at the Casa. She stayed for two weeks. The day she left for a friend's home in California, Fernando asked if they could pray for her. They cried together again.

A week later, Gloria rang them. "I'm phoning you," she said, "because I love you a lot."

God had answered Gloria's prayer when she was in isolation. He led her to Casa de Paz and to Rebeca and Fernando, who witnessed healing through hospitality. It changed us all.

I was getting calls four and five times a day from the guard station at ICE. People were being released that often. Each time, Rebeca and Fernando would walk there, keeping their eyes open for anyone walking the streets carrying a yellow envelope. Not everyone released was willing to wait in the lobby for a stranger to pick them up.

One afternoon, the couple saw three young men ahead of them, two wearing turbans and another who looked Latinx. Fernando called to them. They turned and stared like deer. Then they bolted away in a sprint.

Rebeca and Fernando were startled. "Wait!" Fernando called to them. He ran after them.

They wouldn't stop.

"We're pastors, don't be afraid!" Fernando cried. "We can help you!"

The young Latinx turned around. He called to his friends to come back.

The scene had frightened Rebeca. But mostly, it broke the couple's hearts. When they told me about it, I thought of the verse Fernando quoted: "He had compassion on them, because they were harassed and helpless, like sheep without a shepherd" (Matt. 9:36).

With so many more people being released from detention, Casa de Paz became their safe haven. One night we hosted six guests. Four nationalities sang a song in one voice. The beautiful sound filled Rebeca and Fernando with joy. "You're hoarding this," Rebeca chided me. "This Casa de Paz experience—you have to share it with others."

They opened doors in Mennonite churches for me to speak. Sometimes we all spoke together at a gig. They were as articulate about Casa de Paz as I was. "The church brought us here to help Casa de Paz," Fernando said. "No, no," he gestured emphatically. "It is the opposite. Casa de Paz is helping the church."

Rebeca and Fernando were supposed to stay for two weeks. They stayed for five months. They hosted 117 people. And they heard 117 stories.

"This has changed our vision completely," Fernando told Mennonite congregations. "In the church, we say, 'Raise the money first.' No! Love first. Serve first. Don't open your wallet—open your home, your heart."

The couple were invited to address a group at the University of Colorado in Denver. They were unapologetic with their fellow academics. "Real life is suffering," they said. It was too easy to contain all thought in the realm of theory. "When people lose their families," Fernando said, "they lose themselves."

Meanwhile, Rebeca hammered away with me on a mission statement. I remembered how hard a task it was to shape the right one. We jumpstarted it, but I worked on it for years. It took a long time before I landed on the right phrase: "To reunite families separated by immigrant detention, one simple act of love at a time."

Small acts of love. In the mundane tasks of hosting people, two brilliant minds discovered the profoundest theology. The meaning of compassion expanded for us all.

CHAPTER 9

Dive!

And now these three remain: faith, hope and love.
But the greatest of these is love.

—1 Corinthians 13:13

The gym was freezing. The windows wouldn't close all the way, and snow kept drifting in. It added some unwanted frosting on our necks. It also made the concrete floor seem harder when we dove to dig up the hits. Chins were bouncing off the floor. Most players discovered a hidden strawberry when they got home. But there was one great thing about that first night of Volleyball Internacional: the gym was free.

That last detail is important, because I was broke.

This was my desperate shot at keeping Casa de Paz open: I started a volleyball league.

A pastor knew a pastor who knew a pastor who said we could use his church's gym because he thought it would be a good way to evangelize. That was the agreement for letting me use it. And so in those circumstances, on a winter night at a church gym on West Colfax Avenue, thirty-six bodies slid across freezing concrete wearing more clothes than usual for volleyball.

We played till 2:00 a.m.

Nobody left, because the competition was great. My sister Anna played, thank goodness—fresh from her scholarship stint at Chadron State in Nebraska. There were other players at her level too. It didn't matter that the court had only one net and that four teams had to sit while two played. Nobody left—everybody was *in*. When the clock passed ten, then midnight, then way after, I knew we had a chance. "Tell your friends!" I encouraged everybody as they straggled into the dark.

Maria Caro remembers being smoked by Anna's team. Maria was one of the handful of people who signed up from the radio ad I'd paid for. The competition convinced her she should come back. She knew others would too. Everybody fed off the energy that night.

But people had doubts. Including Maria. She'd heard my short presentation on Casa de Paz—the reason why the league existed. I talked about whom the Casa served and why it mattered. "One hundred percent of your registration fee goes to keep our doors open," I said. "It pays our rent, bills, gas, food, and travel for some guests. Just by playing here tonight, you're helping people affected by immigrant detention."

Maria's curiosity shifted into skepticism. The owner of a cleaning business, she knew how things work. As a teenager, she'd helped run her parents' business because she was the only one who knew English. She learned early how to count dollars and to track exactly where they go. And if she was doing business with someone who looked like me, she learned that it was necessary to have very clear conversations upfront.

"This is all good," she thought that night, "but where is all the money going?" She wasn't the only one in doubt.

The idea started when I hosted a guest at Casa de Paz named Erik. Just after the Christmas holidays—my first at the Casa—he arrived with the warmest smile. He'd been shuttled between several immigrant prisons. Now he sank down into my sofa and cradled a hot coffee. It was his first taste of freedom in four and a half years.

"I got a Christmas card in detention," Erik said. "It was homemade."

"I know who made it!" I exuded. "That was my friend. We all sat right here making those cards."

"Oh, thank you."

"We wanted you to know someone was thinking of you. Were you encouraged?"

"Yes. The number-one thing you can do for us is to care for our souls."

"I'm glad it made a difference."

"There's something else you can do," Erik added. "You can care for our stomachs." I noticed how gaunt he was.

"In detention, you go to sleep hungry," Erik said. "You wake up hungry. You're hungry all day. You're given chores, and you're told, 'If you don't work, you don't eat.'"

I recognized the saying. It was a verse from the Bible, in Timothy, ripped horribly out of context.

"Maybe next year, when you send out those cards," Erik said, "you could include a candy bar or something?"

His words brought to mind another verse: "[If] one of you says to them, 'Go in peace, be warmed and filled,' without giving them the things needed for the body, what good is that?" (James 2:16 ESV).

That was all I needed to hear. I went straight to Kim in the leasing office. We had agreed I would always warn her when I hosted another volunteer party because our gatherings could get pretty animated. She once offered me a bigger apartment with two bedrooms, above the laundry room, and I realized it was because there were no tenants below.

"We're making holiday cards again," I told Kim. "And we're going to include a candy bar."

I must have sounded awfully bold, because I was barely making rent. How was I going to pay for four hundred candy bars?

Less than a year into this, my dollars and cents weren't adding up. Yes, I knew how to stretch a dollar, like any well-trained homeschooler. And yes, I used all of my part-time paycheck from Church Community Builder to pay for Casa's expenses. Now, at the end of every month, I counted pennies as the total of my bank account. One month it was two.

But here's the deal: I couldn't *not* buy fresh food to prepare a starving guest's meal, even if my staple items came from the food pantry. They deserved a decent, quality meal when they got out.

I couldn't *not* buy a bus ticket for a broke dad to get home to his kids in Arkansas. Or Maryland. Or Idaho.

I couldn't *not* use gas to drive him to the bus station downtown.

I couldn't *not* hand a guest a five- or ten-dollar bill for their cross-country bus ride. Some had to travel all the way from Denver to Oregon or Rhode Island. How were they going to make it?

I did have a few nos: No, I would not ask people for money. No, I would never go into the red. No, I would not spend a cent on myself that came in for Casa de Paz. And no, I would never apply for government grants. I wanted to eliminate every barrier a person might have to connect with an immigrant. I wanted to be able to say to everyone, "None of your tax dollars goes toward what I do."

And so, toward the end of every month, I had to eat a few meals at Metro Caring's soup kitchen. I wore my clothes an extra day or two—or three or four—when I didn't have quarters to do laundry.

I'm an anxious person, but I keep my problems to myself. I

use anxiety as fuel, filling out my daily list of things to cross off. But at day's end, when the last item disappears, I don't wring my hands. I'm a realist; I know when I've done everything I can. So the time came when I told myself I had to shut it all down.

"No mas," I told my new boyfriend. "It was a good idea, wasn't it?"

I think I surprised him. He knew I didn't quit easily. I'd just spent three years of my life trying to make something happen. "Hold on," he said, "can you do something else to pay the bills?"

He knew I couldn't take on another job.

"No, I mean can you make money doing something fun? Something you spend time doing anyway?"

Like?

"Volleyball. You like volleyball. *Latinos* like volleyball." He was Latino. He knew of which he spoke.

Hmm. "Maybe I could start a league?"

"You could market to Latinos."

"There must already be tons of Latinx leagues. People could just google them."

"It doesn't work that way with us," he said. "We'll join a league if our friend tells us about it. Or if we drive by and see a cousin playing. We need a comfortable place to play."

I had to beg my friends to show up to play that first night. When I placed a radio ad on a Spanish station, I got exactly three calls from it. Then somehow those three calls turned into ten signups. Enough for two teams—if my boyfriend and I played. You can't make a league out of that; you can't even have a tournament! So we called all our friends, and we got just enough players to fill six rosters.

Brittney Compton was one of the higher-level players who showed up. She isn't Latinx—she looks typically Scandinavian and typically made for volleyball. She played at Front Range Christian School in Littleton, the south suburb where she grew up. But she was drawn to Volleyball Internacional because of her affinity for Latin culture. She'd recently started a job as a registered dietitian with WIC—Women, Infants, and Children—the federal nutritional health program to assist struggling families. It's run by the Department of Agriculture and directs young families to community resources for a healthy start. Brittney was intrigued by my presentation about Casa de Paz.

"I'd like to come see what you're doing," she said. I knew right away she had a big heart for vulnerable people. The day she came to the Casa, my guest was an anxious Nepalese young woman who was so tiny she looked like a teenager. "She won't sleep with the lights off," I whispered. Brittney was moved.

Situations like this woman's were starting to get to me. I walked into the ICE lobby to see if anyone was released and noticed a Latinx woman in her seventies. She had some kind of leg injury, and I had to help her to her feet. She grimaced with every step on the short walk to Casa de Paz. I couldn't believe this—somebody's freakin' grandmother was *imprisoned?*

These were mistreatments by a broken, unjust immigration system. Yet the real horror show was what people endured *before* they arrived in the US. I thought I'd heard every story. I hadn't. Every tale was different—from men and women, old and young, from every continent—tales of being raped, beaten, chased by attackers with machetes; tales of kidnappings and children held at gunpoint. All told in sober, tearful pain by guest after guest after guest.

Yet for families who came to visit a loved one in detention, every story was the same: A hardworking loved one arrested and deported. Spouses missing each other. Kids longing for their moms or dads. Everywhere I turned in the apartment, I saw suffering: Someone sitting on the couch downcast, rubbing her hands anxiously. Someone sitting solemnly at the dining table, unable to tolerate more than a few bites after a long prison diet of gruel.

Someone leaning on the balcony railing outside my door, staring into the courtyard, alone in his memory of a relative butchered by a cartel. No guest ever had shoelaces. ICE confiscated them to prevent suicides. A young Bangladeshi we visited at ICE wasn't able to sleep. He'd fled a radical faction of the Muslim political party, which had beaten him severely for siding with the opposition. He had endured two years in detention without a visitor until our volunteer came along. He begged the volunteer to come see him again; otherwise, he was afraid he would end his life.

The suffering didn't stop. It was there day after day after day. It was never *not* there.

Good people suffering. And Christians being indifferent, focusing on lawbreaking, at times being hateful.

Why? Why? Why?

Growing up, there were always answers. We sang, "God is omnipresent, God is all love." Where was that God in the reality I saw every day? How could he know about all these tragedies and not be heartbroken as I was? How could he be all love if the world he made was full of endless horrors? What all-powerful God wouldn't act to stop it? My dad would leap on a plane to help me if these things were happening to me. My mom would stand in front of a train to protect me. They would give their lives for me. Did God give up on the people I hosted?

I had gone into this work thinking God led me into it. Now I wondered whether God existed. He couldn't. Not in this world. Not if these kinds of horrors had gone on forever.

My anger grew. And grew. And grew. But I wasn't angry at God. There *was* no God. There couldn't be.

Something happened that I once would have considered a miracle. ICE called saying a guy was about to be released, but he had a leg injury. They wouldn't let him go unless he had a wheelchair. Could we provide one?

I put out a request on Facebook. Someone at Jude Del Hierro's ministry texted me: "We just had a wheelchair donated— *yesterday*. We've never had a wheelchair in all our fifteen years."

Things like that kept me going.

The next week at volleyball, I brought a surprise guest. Rodrigo was the guest who needed the wheelchair; he was healing at Casa de Paz and now could walk with a leg brace. A gregarious guy, Rodrigo had everyone laughing over tales of my ramshackle hospitality. I reminded everybody, "By playing in this league, you're supporting people like Rodrigo."

Little did I know, Rodrigo's appearance that night started a sea change at Volleyball Internacional.

This is real! Maria Caro thought when she heard him. She knew guys like Rodrigo. No more second-guessing where league fees went. She looked around and saw the other skeptics buying in too.

A petite young woman who played that night was amused that I'd opened my presentation with a prayer. She was cool with it, hearing it as a thankful kind of thing. Andrea had a shy smile that lit up the gym and a competitor's fire that left burns on the concrete floor. But something stuck with her too about seeing Rodrigo.

Andrea had been only eight when she crossed the Texas border from Mexico with her mother and younger brother. All she remembers is being wakened while it was still dark and hugging her grandmother goodbye, then holding her mom's hand and being led along in the cold. They crossed a port of entry with temporary visas, to reunite with their dad, who was in Colorado. Months later, when the visas expired, the family did what sixty percent of "undocumented" people living in the US today did: they stayed.

Growing up, Andrea was unaware of the stakes of living undocumented. She awakened to them a few years later, in the circular drive around Park Meadows Shopping Mall, south of Denver. The family van was stopped by a cop. Andrea's dad was driving, and her mom dissolved into a panic. Thankfully, they weren't cited for anything, but Andrea had never seen that kind of fear in her mother. It opened the door to her understanding.

Nowadays, hearing a story like Rodrigo's could bring back that moment for her. As she looked around the gym, she knew there were other stories like hers. It was a mixed night: great volleyball and a flash of pain.

She went home and told her boyfriend, Josh.

"This girl does *what?*"

Josh was intrigued by the idea of Casa de Paz. Also the volleyball league. "A league that does *what* for Mexicans?"

Andrea grinned. "Not Mexicans. *Internacional.* Anybody can come."

Josh is as tall and rangy as Andrea is petite. He was skeptical. "I'm going with you next week."

Andrea and Josh are like many couples in the US—one a processed first-generation immigrant, the other a citizen by birth. (In one out of every five couples in the US, one partner is foreign-born.) Both are athletes. Both are big weekend hikers. And both work administratively in the medical field—Andrea at one of Denver's largest hospitals, Josh at a chain of public-health clinics. Yet like so many couples, theirs is a tale of two very different histories.

Josh's dad is a tough-as-nails, native-born Texan. He had shuttled between Juarez and El Paso in his work as a firefighter before scoring work in the Denver area, where he and Josh's mom raised their family. Young Josh grew up knowing what detention centers are. Their family knew people in the neighborhood who'd been detained.

"The cops are good guys," Josh's dad taught. "If you get stopped, respect them. Act normal. Act like a citizen, because you *are* a citizen."

"What about my uncles?" Josh asked. Two of them had spent a little time in jail. "They did time because they did something wrong!" his dad emphasized.

The threat of detention meant something different to Andrea's family. They were from an area near Mexico City, where her dad worked for the postal service but was also an entrepreneur. He owned a pharmacy, a gift shop, and a burger joint. Once in the US, he wanted to start a taco truck. But to get started, first he had to work for someone who would hire him without status papers.

A small company hired both of Andrea's parents, and they were great employees. But the boss was caught and cited for hiring undocumented people. He could avoid trouble, though, by cutting a deal. He had to supply a fall guy—meaning, one of the undocumented workers. He chose Andrea's mom.

She was jailed for two weeks. It crushed the family. Andrea and her brother were frightened, and their dad was crippled with anguish. The spirit of the household changed.

Josh knew about this kind of "alternative justice" forced on Andrea's family. He grew up respecting authority, but he also saw how average people experienced injustice. The dual reality caused Josh to question everything. Like Andrea, he excelled academically and was interested in medical work. He played football at Coe College in Iowa, where he studied biology and worked on cadavers. He dropped out his senior year, mainly because it was too expensive, but he was also uncomfortable with the track he was on. It seemed too elite; he was vigilant about staying clear-eyed in life. So he came back to Denver and started work for Metro Care Provider Network, the public-health clinics. It suited him well, because he got a ground-level view of people's needs.

"So after volleyball next week," he told Andrea, "maybe we can do that other thing. Casa de Paz." His own eyes would tell him whether the "girl" running these things was in it for money.

I got a call from Maria Caro. "I have a suggestion for your league," she said. "You might want to start your games a little later. I have friends who want to come, but they work construction till six. You probably have other players in their situation."

She was clueing me in to who my constituency was. And I loved it. Maria and I clicked on business. I asked her to keep the ideas coming. By the next round of signups, we had ten teams instead of six.

We moved to a different gym, at a Jewish school, because it had more courts. And we'd made enough money to pay the league's expenses and Casa's too. It was working.

Yet while things were on the way up for Casa de Paz, my faith was on a downward slide. All the way down.

For me, if there was no God, it meant that nothing mattered. And so I let a lot of things go. Someone overheard me swearing and asked, "You losing your religion, Sarah?" I'd never realized that phrase meant being super angry—which in my case was accurate. And also literal about losing faith. The anger I carried drove me to one of two conclusions: (1) I didn't believe there was a God who would allow all of this suffering or (2) if there was a God, all the suffering I was seeing was not cool.

I chose the first. And I threw off every restraint I'd been taught as a Christian. I did a deep dive into everything that a

Christian didn't do. Everything except getting drunk. Nothing worse to me than puke laced with alcohol. Aagh!

Old truths I'd been taught came back to me in angering ways. Like the saying, "Everything happens for a reason"—as if atrocities were destined to happen to people. No, no, no.

Or, "Be thankful in all things." I couldn't live by that. It cheapened faith to say I'm thankful for good things if I couldn't say I'm thankful when horrible things happened. And I couldn't.

I stopped talking about God and Jesus as if they existed. I used phrases like "higher power" or "something bigger than us."

I kept thinking of Anton's words: *Be willing to rethink some things about what you believe. In fact, maybe everything you know about God.*

Sorry. It was hard for me to even entertain the idea of God.

Be willing to suffer with people.

That was hard too. But that I could do.

At volleyball, I was learning some players' everyday burdens. "My brother wants to come here 'the right way,'" a guy told me. "Do you know how long the wait is for a sibling from Mexico? Twelve years. And if he waits till next year to get in line, it'll be more than that. The line gets longer all the time."

People felt free to tell their stories within the community. To share their burdens. And the volleyball unified them even more. I looked forward to every Wednesday night at the gym, because there was release and joy. It was like salsa in that way. I especially loved it when families played together. One couple brought their teenage daughter with them every week. To me, that was the best.

Also like salsa: I got hit on by guys at volleyball. That was inevitable. But nothing there was ever going to happen. Not because I had a boyfriend, because I didn't anymore. We had broken up. After that, I just wanted to keep the lines clean between business and personal life. After all, I still had to be the bad cop in a competitive league.

I hadn't been asked out by a white guy in a while. The one time I was, I asked him to go salsa dancing. As soon as we walked in, one of the Latinx regulars saw me and asked me to dance. I jumped at the invitation, and we cumbia'd and bounced through several songs—okay, more than a couple—and when we finished, my date was gone. I was totally cool with it.

Ditching him was a horrible thing to do. But I had a lot of anger going on. And it had nothing to do with the color of a guy's skin. This too had to do with God.

I had once been in a serious Christian relationship. Very serious—the kind that you and your entire community agree is bonded by God and that you all assume will last a lifetime. The kind of relationship you build on with an eye toward *forever*. And because you stand on all of these things, you allow grace toward faults and failures, until those things become abuses, and those abuses finally go over a line. And then, in an instant, everything you had put your faith in, including the bond you thought God had put there, shatters. And you shatter.

After that kind of devastation, the pure release of salsa is a gift. On the night I ditched my date, I wasn't ready for a go-slow, tied-down kind of dating. I probably never should have accepted when the guy asked me out. I wasn't looking for a relationship. I was still looking to be free of something painful.

At volleyball, getting involved with someone wasn't going to be good business. But it worked for my sister! Funny, because Anna thought she was done with dating. Then somebody told her she needed to try Tinder, the dating app. She did—and her first match was with a guy from Volleyball Internacional!

"What?!" I screamed. "That tall guy, I'll bet. Latinx?"

Javier is gracious and soft-spoken, but with enough male pride to disagree with Anna over who made the first move. All I know is, they both swiped right on Tinder.

My brother-in-law is one fabulous guy. Like his mom, he's

a librarian, with a steady temperament. Javier's a perfect match for my sister, who had to handle rowdy juveniles in her day job. And to my utter joy, in just a few years' time, he and my sister gave me the world's greatest gift. Ever.

By season three, Volleyball Internacional had grown to twenty teams. We moved to Dive, a gym on the northeast side of Denver. It had four courts, so eight teams could play simultaneously. I had to ask players to referee between their own games. They got a taste of the whining I handled.

"I was only two minutes late," was an excuse I heard a gazillion times. "Yes," I said. "You were two minutes late." That always rankled them.

Maria Caro gave me some advice: "Late is okay in the culture. Think about giving a little leeway."

She came to me about something else: "Sarah, you have got to make people pay their fees. I hear them saying they forgot their wallet, and you say they can pay next time. No! 'You pay next time? You *play* next time.'"

I got her point. "But I don't want to turn off anybody about Casa de Paz."

"That's all lost money *for* the Casa!" Maria said. "It takes an enforcer. Why don't you let me do it? I can take the heat off you."

She was great at managing that, of course. And I made her accept more payment than she wanted to. Even a no-nonsense businesswoman like Maria was in it for the Casa.

Best of all, she freed me up to do more leadership at Casa de Paz. Which I needed to do, because players were coming straight from the gym to volunteer at the Casa. One night, it was Andrea and Josh.

They got to meet a memorable guest from West Africa.

Winston was an exceptional cook and had prepared a wonderful dinner for the other guests. He pulled out the leftovers and invited Josh and Andrea to sit and eat while he told them about his long journey to the US. Winston operated in the kitchen with the swagger of a champion athlete, which he was as an elite squash player who compete all over Africa. He also excelled in the ribbing that competitors do with one another, and we all were game for it. He left a promising professional career when he had to flee his strife-torn country. Now an asylee, he would start work to bring his wife and toddler son to the US.

Josh was blown away. He'd thought everyone in detention was from Mexico. And he'd never heard a journey like this guy's—all the way up from South America.

"We have another guest downstairs who's getting ready to leave on a bus," I said as Andrea and Josh finished their dinner. "Could you guys take him to the station?"

As the couple drove along, the man from rural Latin America in their back seat marveled at every sight. He pointed to a stoplight and asked what it was. "I feel like I am in a dream," he said. "A good dream."

Nothing that evening was what Josh expected. He'd known about detention since he was a kid, but this didn't match what he assumed from those years. He kept wondering, *Why haven't I ever given this any thought?*

As they waved goodbye to the man boarding his bus, Andrea texted me. "Josh says, 'Tell Sarah I'll do anything to help. I want to donate. And I want to play for her.'"

The league took on a life of its own. If a volleyball regular didn't show up for a week or two, everyone wanted to know why. Texts and calls went out with caring concern.

Daniel Ponce de Leon was playing one night when a team-mate showed up in tears: her brother had been detained. There were two hundred people in the gym; within minutes, everyone knew about it. Between games, players embraced the grieving sister. I was about to make my usual presentation on Casa de Paz when I felt a tap on my shoulder. A guy had gone to his car and brought back a jar. "Can we ask people to give?" he asked. "To raise something for her brother's bond?"

Daniel and I talked often about the deep bond in the league. "There's trust and commitment to each other," he pointed out. "When we say we'll support each other, we do it."

One night, I saw an entire new team stride in wearing uniforms. "Whoa, who's that?" I asked Maria Caro.

"That's my friend," she said. "His team was playing in a different league. I told him about Casa de Paz, and he pulled them out to come play here. They'd rather support the Casa."

Skeptical newcomers still had questions whenever I made my presentation about the Casa. Their doubts were addressed by the veterans. "Have you been to Casa de Paz, bro?" Josh would ask them. "Do you see where she lives?" Andrea would ask them, "Have you walked in her shoes?" And Maria was Maria. She spoke with all the authority of a Latinx mom. And you don't mess with the Latinx mom.

When nothing matters, you have no purpose. I drifted along for months feeling there was no point to anything. Including the wild stuff I'd thrown myself into. Nothing satisfied. I finally stopped it all. I was just wasting time.

I took my questions about God to people I respected. They were like me—they didn't have answers, either. They ended up being the most helpful to me, because they didn't try to explain it all. It's one thing to have a head knowledge of theology. It's another to see, touch, and taste the suffering of guests in your home day after day.

It helped that others were seeing it along with me. Andrea and Josh were at the Casa one night when a guest from El Salvador needed to get to relatives in Florida. "Should I call your family," I asked, "to see if they can buy you a plane ticket?"

"Bus," he said.

"Are you sure?" Josh asked. "That's a twenty-two-hour trip. Wouldn't you rather fly?" The man was adamant. He had flown only twice in his life, he said—both times on ICE Air. Like everyone else on those flights, he was shackled hands to feet in his seat, facing the floor and unable to raise himself up. Everyone rode that way. For hours at a time. The cabin filled with the smell of urine and excrement.

Josh and Andrea also were there the night we hosted Luna, a tiny indigenous Mayan from Guatemala. She spoke Mam, the indigenous language, which doesn't break into sentences but continues in one long expression. Her group is belittled as the country's despised minority, and Luna's story was brutal. Robbers had killed her baby son in front of her. Luna couldn't report the murder, because police won't help Mayans.

Coming north to safety, Luna nearly died trying to cross the US border with a group of men in a cold, dangerous mountain area near El Paso. Josh is a vigorous outdoorsy guy, and even he wouldn't have tried spending the night in that area. He was astounded that frail Luna survived. She almost didn't; she woke in the dark, woozy, weak, and naked. The men had raped her and left.

Luna saw her torn clothes strewn nearby. She could barely move. Weakly, she cried for help. Border Patrol agents picked up her sound signals on a tracking device. Getting caught saved Luna's life.

Her story rocked Andrea. They were the same age.

Luna was excited about going to the airport. "It's my fourth plane trip!" she enthused. That broke Josh's and Andrea's hearts; they knew her other three flights were on ICE Air.

Another Guatemalan guest that night fretted over her own bus trip. Patricia, a Spanish speaker of the dominant culture, faced a fifty-two-hour bus ride to the East Coast with no money. She didn't know how she would eat for the next two days.

"Here, Patricia," Luna said, producing a ten-dollar bill from her backpack. Josh and Andrea knew that was all Luna had. If she'd had more, she would have given it too.

Evenings like that one changed the way Josh looked at his job in the health clinics. Whenever he worked a front desk, he listened closer to where a client was from. "I understand," he reassured them, hiding his melting heart. "Let me help you with this."

Andrea's lingering pain became compassion. She was a patient financial advocate at St. Joseph's, the large hospital near Denver's City Park. She assisted people on limited incomes, presenting discounts and sliding-scale costs through the state-funded Colorado Indigent Care Program. But undocumented people were always reluctant to get treatment unless they were desperately sick. Their first question was always, "How will this affect our residency?" Andrea explained that they didn't have to worry about that, that the law protected their status. But she understood their reluctance. She knew the feeling all too well.

Brittney Compton started giving rides to Casa guests. That had its challenges too. She called me after taking an African guy to the airport.

"He asked me to marry him," she said. We laughed. "I wanted

to make sure he arrived okay in California, so when he asked for my number I gave it to him. I know that was risky. I hope it doesn't go against your policy."

Um, *policy?* I was doing everything on the fly. I didn't have an answer for her. I only knew what I would do for myself, and that wasn't always advisable for everyone else.

It had never occurred to me to ask whether our volunteers were safe with all our guests or whether anyone we hosted had a criminal record. I couldn't say. But I found out we had a rock-solid protection behind that question: the warden's assistant was looking out for me. Aurora ICE has an area called Level Three, where people with serious criminal records are held. He never told those guys about Casa de Paz.

Only one guest I ever hosted at the Casa over the years seemed a bit off. The guy turned out to have a chronic mental health issue. Detention had worsened his condition. I called his lawyer to come for him, and that was that.

Brittney had another uniquely "Casa moment" when she picked up three Sikh men just released from detention. She saw them carrying ICE envelopes and trying to board a bus near the railroad tracks, but the driver wouldn't let them on. So she pulled to the curb and somehow convinced them to let her give them a ride to the Casa. Instead, they gave her the address of a Sikh temple in Commerce City, a northeast surburb of Denver.

The drive to the temple went through mile after mile of countryside, with no lights under a black winter's night sky. After a half hour of driving, Brittney was momentarily unnerved until she realized the men in her car must have been too. Finally, they came upon a majestic structure rising from the horizon of the flat prairie. The temple attendants who answered the door insisted that Brittney stay for dinner along with the three guests she'd delivered. The food was gourmet quality, Brittney later told me. Better, we both admitted, than what she would have had at

Casa de Paz! The trip to the temple became a regular route for our volunteers. None of them ever complained about the food.

We ran out of pillows. I kept giving them to guests who had to take long bus rides. One night there wasn't a single pillow left in the Casa.

The next day, a woman from a church stopped by. She was carrying a clear pack of brand-new, bright-white pillows. "Could you use these, Sarah?"

Okay, it was another wheelchair moment. I'd been taught to pay attention to these kinds of things as a homeschooler.

I stacked up the pillows and took a picture. I didn't want to forget this. I told my mom about it. "It's not a coincidence," she said.

In my spiritual condition, I couldn't bring myself to agree— not out loud, anyway. But deep down, a part of me wanted to say, "You're right."

Maybe things do happen right on time.

Maria Caro and I did a lot of late-night brainstorming for volleyball. I drew on some of the practices I'd learned at Church Community Builder. We printed thank-you cards for the volleyball players, with info about Casa de Paz and an extra registration form. The cards always brought in a second friend. And we shared real heartaches. By the end of the first year, three players had been detained. The community always rallied, raising money through raffles and extra tournaments. It was personal. My life and my work were no longer just about coming alongside strangers. It was about my friends.

Word gets around quickly in any tightly knit community. I shouldn't have been surprised when a journalist from Univision came to play one night. "I'd heard about this, but I needed to see for myself," he said, taking in the gym's scene. "Would you mind if I brought a crew?"

Would I mind?!

He interviewed Edgar, a torture survivor from Latin America. Yet the journalist's own immigration story was as harrowing as anyone's. His reporting in Mexico earned him death threats from the cartels. He had to emigrate to the US.

My Spanish wasn't perfect on camera, but I was fluent enough for a three-minute spot as volleyballs whizzed past my head. I sent out an email for everyone to watch when it aired. I imagined all the players around town watching that night: They saw their community's story—not just volleyball but their flesh and blood. Their pain and strength were no longer in the shadows.

And it encouraged others who needed it even more: people detained in ICE. When I showed up in the lobby one day, a guy just released pointed to me and said, "You're the TV lady." He gestured back to the pods. "We all watched you!" Everyone inside knew a league existed just for them.

"You are now the Spanish face of Casa de Paz," I told Andrea. 9News and Fox31 had done features on us after Univision did. Now Telemundo was calling. Andrea had great presence. Her TV smile was tailor-made for this.

A seat was reserved for Casa de Paz on a panel at Denver's annual Latinas LEAD Power Summit. I asked Andrea, "Can you go? You'll be representin' the Casa."

That year the event was at the magnificent Buell Theatre at Denver's downtown arts complex. One by one, Latina leaders strode to the podium and spoke. Andrea was excited to be among them, but with every speaker, she felt a cloud forming over her heart. As she listened to their difficult stories, she thought, *They're telling mine.*

She had excelled academically. She was on track with a state program that helps kids get to college. She hit the books hard and fist-pumped every achievement. Now she wanted to put some hours into community service for her resume. She wanted to go to the best university possible because she was going to be a doctor.

Children's Hospital in Denver was world renowned; that's where she would apply to volunteer. The paperwork to do that was pretty extensive. On the day of her interview, her mom drove her. As the interviewer looked through Andrea's application, she nodded affirmingly. Then she looked concerned. "There's something missing," she said. "We need your Social Security number."

No. That meant they would do a screening background check. Her undocumented status would be discovered.

It was over.

Andrea looked into the interviewer's eyes and her world crumbled. She and her mom left. Andrea cried the whole day. It didn't matter how perfect a record she achieved. She wasn't going to make a life here. All the work she'd done—none of it would matter to anyone. It was already in the trash.

She wasn't eligible for scholarships. She wasn't eligible for loans. She didn't want to clean offices using someone else's Social Security number. She wanted to go back to Mexico. She asked her dad to start looking for colleges there for her.

Andrea eventually went to college in the US. The same year she interviewed to volunteer at Children's Hospital, she qualified for a U visa. Those are special visas for people who've suffered substantial mental or physical abuse. Andrea had been sexually assaulted at age thirteen. A few years had passed since the incident, but she still qualified. That U visa allowed her—and her family—to stay in the United States. She went to Metro State, the university in downtown Denver.

"We lived undocumented for a long time," she told her Latina Summit listeners. "On my job, I talk to undocumented people all the time. They're scared. You watch them as they try to fill out an application. It's the hardest thing for them. They don't even want to leave the room to get water. They're afraid something will happen, that one of them will be taken.

"If you're born here, you live in a bubble. You don't know. You can't fully appreciate it. My job allows me never to forget what it was like.

"Everyone who's a guest at Casa de Paz has a story they're running away from. As a volunteer, you listen, you learn, you understand. And you're thankful. For me personally, doing the work of Casa de Paz is part of my own inner work.

"I grew up thinking I knew what I wanted to do. And then something happened, and everything clicked. Sarah Jackson, our founder, said a beautiful thing: 'Things always happen at the right time.' It's true, everything comes into your life when you're finally ready. Not early, not late. Just on time.

"Nothing comes easily, but I continue looking for things that motivate me and remind me why I am doing what I do. Casa de Paz came into my life at the right time, when I knew that being a doctor wasn't happening for me. Sarah's passion and love for this organization and this cause always reminds me that there are bigger things. Casa de Paz is one of them."

Okay, God. Maybe I'll rethink things. Rethink you.

At a certain age when you're young in your faith, a lot of teaching has to do with surrendering something to God. I never thought I would have to surrender my belief to God. When it became hard to believe, I just decided there must not be a God.

A guest at the Casa explained to me how he held on to hope despite everything. "If you cannot fly, you run. If you cannot run, you walk. If you cannot walk, you crawl," he said between bites of my spaghetti. "But whatever you do, *keep going*."

One night I picked up a man at ICE. I asked him, "So, after everything you've been through, did you think it was safe to get into a car with a stranger?"

"I knew that God would make it safe," he said.

Two men arrived at the Casa one evening, a Muslim and a Catholic. Both wanted to know if there were places they could go to worship. They wanted to give thanks to God for freeing them.

Another Muslim guest left us this thank-you note: "We can't pay you, but we can pray for you, from every angle."

Everywhere I turned in the Casa, I was surrounded by gratitude. By hope. By worship. Yes, there was still suffering and awful trauma. But people gave thanks for simple things—the sun on their skin, a private shower, a decent meal, the use of a phone—things I take for granted every day.

A guest once told me, "You should call this place 'Casa de Esperanza.' It gives such hope."

I still had no answers. Neither did anyone I knew. Yet my parents still had faith. My guests still had faith. And their families still had faith. So I decided to trust the people around me. I had only the faith of others, and it was powerful to me. They were the ones suffering; I wasn't the one getting the worst end of things. They helped me see that struggle is part of life. And thus my guests helped me remember my God. I respected their faith. If they, who had been through so much, could still believe, so could I.

I gazed around one night at volleyball, and all four courts were full and going. The gym was filled with people letting their hair down (or rather putting it up in ponytails), enjoying themselves, enjoying each other. I saw friendships that hadn't existed before. Bonds that went deep. Unspoken support—the kind you can count on if you ever need anything.

I felt something I hadn't in a long time: pride. Deep, satisfying pride. I'd set up a business, something to provide an income for a cause, and it had become much more than that.

"Pass. Set. Hit. Reunite." That became our tagline. We ran our business to the needs of the players, and now we'd grown to fill out the entire Dive gym. Four divisions, sixty players in each, seven-week seasons, tournament at the end. We handed out prizes. ("Medals," Josh insisted, "the prizes have to be medals. For Latinx, it's about bragging rights!") We had pizza parties. We had special nights. And families were reunited—on the court and in detention—through Casa de Paz.

All of Casa's bills were being paid, and then some. We could buy plane tickets more often for guests who had a long way to travel. And not only that, by year's end, we had saved nearly $5,000.

The league was stable. "It's fine if we stay at this size," I told Maria. She agreed. We were meeting the needs of the Casa de Paz community. It wasn't about growing a business; the business was about growing support for people.

Amid that success, one question was never far from any player's mind: "What happens if one of us gets deported?" It has never stopped being asked.

You can never stop loving your neighbor. *Keep going, whatever you do*—because you never know who's playing beside you. What story they carry. And how much alike you are.

I ask more questions now, at thirty-five years old, than I ever have. And I know the least amount in my life. I was glad I went through my dark period. It's okay to wonder. What if I knew all the answers, anyway? What difference would it make? What would I do differently?

I finally told myself, I'm just going to believe again. Where is the harm in that? What's the worst that could happen if I believe?

It's like asking, "Is it better to cry or to laugh? Better to get super angry, or to let my hair down and dance?"

Why not do both? I went to salsa whenever I got the chance. It was one of those good and perfect gifts. And I remembered the source of that kind of gift, oh so well.

PART 4

A Race To Run

God's love tears down walls. No longer religion
against religion, Christians against non-
Christians, but justice against sin, life against
death. Therefore, every person you encounter
should be your concern. Do not settle for less.

—CHRISTOPH FRIEDRICH BLUMHARDT, *Everyone Belongs to God*

CHAPTER 10

For Such a Time

*Do not forget to show hospitality to strangers, for
by so doing some people have shown hospitality to
angels without knowing it.*

—HEBREWS 13:2

There's a party on earth that I know is seen from heaven. It's been ongoing for years, and it takes place in a house in northeast Denver. Every night at this party, a new arrival is celebrated. They're received like returning family, with hugs and handshakes, a home-cooked meal, a bed made for them with a fluffed pillow and a square of chocolate and a handwritten note. The note, inscribed by one of the dozens of partygoers who come each night, reminds the guest how glad everyone is they've arrived, how welcome they are, and that now, with their presence, the party is complete.

This ongoing party is, paradoxically, a "reunion of strangers." People with seemingly nothing in common connect in the commonest ways. They discover almost immediately that, really, they have *everything* in common. When a guest arrives, they're summoned to a seat at the beautifully spread dinner table. They're handed a phone so they can let their loved ones know where they are and that they're safe. They're doted on, fussed over as they're served a handcrafted dish prepared with them in mind. Later, as the celebration winds down, they're shown a comfortable bedroom where they can relax for the evening and a sparkling bathroom where they can take a soothing shower to let down after a long journey. The next day, they're handed a travel ticket so they can go to the arms of their loved ones, friends, families, and sponsors living in the US. And they're supplied with helpful gifts for their journey homeward.

This great party is well known even by people who've never been to it. I remember once when a disoriented man, abruptly released from immigrant prison, made his way to downtown Denver. He walked five and a half miles, carrying an ICE-issued garbage bag filled with his belongings. Everyone must have thought he was homeless; most people glanced away. Finally, someone pointed him to the Denver Rescue Mission, where he would be taken in. Yet before he entered the Mission door, a friendly stranger stopped him. "You belong somewhere else," the stranger advised. That stranger drove him fifteen miles to our house—to the great, nightly, ongoing party at Casa de Paz, dropping him at the curb and driving away.

We were puzzled as our guest told us this story. We thought maybe the kind driver was a Casa de Paz volunteer or someone in our network. How did he know our address? "He never told me," said our guest. "I don't know how I got here or who brought me." For the first time, I thought maybe an angel had delivered someone to the Casa's door.

We were just as surprised by another unlikely referral. "How did you hear about us?" a Casa volunteer asked our African guest. "The judge told me," the guest answered. "When I won my case, he said, 'I know a very good place you can go.'" It was the first time I'd heard of an immigration judge referring someone to Casa de Paz.

Six years after we opened our doors, we had lots of stories to celebrate. And so, on one special evening—the fourth Friday of April 2018—a dozen or so people gathered in the living room of our new home, a bilevel ranch house rented to us at mortgage cost by the generous owner, Jesús. Thanks to Volleyball Internacional—maxed out at eighty teams—we could afford it. So many league players were jacked up about the new house that on moving day they brought trucks and muscle to make it happen.

I was thrilled to have a real casa, no longer just an apartment: two bedrooms upstairs, one for me and one for Casa's faithful live-in volunteer Winston. I knew from his dedicated character, easygoing nature, and unflagging faith that he would be the perfect support person for the Casa, covering for me as my speaking schedule grew. I also could tell from his sly sense of humor that he could survive my meltdowns!

The basement was outfitted with three bedrooms, one for families, one for women guests and one for men, two pairs of bunk beds in each. Everybody at the Casa could be comfortable now. For half a decade I had shared space with more and more guests, sometimes ten people altogether with a single bathroom. Winston and I often slept on blankets on the floor. Now we each had privacy. It was a well-earned reward for a hardworking man like him with a day job as well as Casa responsibilities. As for me, having a room of my own did wonders for my work, my privacy (boundaries again!), and my state of mind about the Casa.

This special night, under an azure-canopied April sky, was our monthly potluck, a practice I started so that our 175 active volunteers could meet each other. Casa de Paz reached into so many different communities that people came from all over the city—and all walks of life—to help. Yet the highlight of every monthly potluck was the guests' arrival. That spring evening, as eight newly released men ascended the bilevel stairs, the packed living room erupted in applause.

My eyes filled at the sound of it. Eight guests, surely wide-eyed, the objects of someone's joy after years of feeling scorn.

I didn't get to see their glorious reception. I was forced to listen from the next room. Three years after a serious stress diagnosis, I was bedridden with another mysterious illness. This one had me nauseated nonstop. Maybe a symptom of my resurging perfectionism with Casa's growth? After my stress diagnosis, I'd asked my mom, "Am I a perfectionist?" She tilted her head sympathetically. "Is that a joke?"

I was just happy I hadn't missed the potluck. It was one of Casa de Paz's best nights ever. Debbie, one of our very first Menno volunteers, described everything to me in an email. The guests were from seven countries—Cameroon, Belarus, Venezuela, Indonesia, Eritrea, Chechnya, and Pakistan. They sat down to a steaming dinner of chicken and rice. Their ICE-issued garbage bags were replaced by backpacks stocked with snacks, bottled water, toiletries, and travel essentials. Volunteers riffled through the downstairs clothing bins to provide one guest with a belt, another with socks, others with coats and sweaters. During dinner, each guest was handed a cell phone donated to the Casa to help them with travel. Meanwhile, several volunteers labored in our attached garage, quietly sorting donations. Activity like this went on every weeknight, every week of the year.

On the surface, the most mundane things were happening: a dinner, chores, practicalities. And yet seated at our table were eight profound personal histories. How much suffering was represented by those eight bowed heads? How many years or decades of perseverance and faith in detention could be added up around that table? The rest of us took for granted the simple pleasures those eight men now enjoyed: a hot meal, a warm shower, freedom to walk outside and stare up at the sky. Very few of us volunteers could fathom the significance of these evenings. But those men did. And so did heaven.

Two volunteer groups showed up that night for the potluck. A pair of teachers from a local elementary school brought a banner their students made to encourage our guests. A knitting group brought caps and gloves they'd made for any guests traveling to cold climates. They joined a growing cadre of Casa supporters scattered across the Front Range, from churches to breweries to professionals to retirees to groups like Warm Cookies of the Revolution and a punk-band-fronting immigration lawyer and one very enthusiastic volunteer experiencing homelessness. I wonder if they know they're all part of a great historical stream.

Debbie didn't have to describe the next part of the evening. I heard it through the wall—an ebullient voice of authority booming gratitude to everyone present.

"Thank you for what you are doing," said Celestine Tatung. His legal skill had helped win freedom for our two Cameroonian guests. "We got two out today, and we'll get another out tomorrow," he declared, to more whoops and applause. He and his wife, Elizabeth, had won hundreds of cases for immigrants through their Maryland-based practice. Because the Tatungs are originally from Cameroon, no one appreciates the US's rule of law more than they do. Both were due to fly out early the next morning for court appearances, he in Los Angeles, she in Atlanta.

Celestine pointed to his two clients. "They were in a bad situation, a country close to civil war," he noted. "If Anthony was not here tonight, he would be dead. If Clive went back there, they would kill him. I tell you, friends, Someone is watching. That is where your reward comes from."

So many people shared in the great reward Celestine invoked. To volunteers, that reward was the privilege of hosting the guests. To others, it was the opportunity to serve. A philanthropy group sent a crew to build a wall in the basement creating a women's bedroom for privacy. Frank, a neighbor down the street and a skilled contractor, offered handiwork if we needed it. A Catholic volunteer named Pat came the next week to repair our back deck. I never imagined having a grassy back yard for Casa guests, much less a redwood platform where they could soak in Colorado's beautiful sunshine. Later that month, for the Casa's sixth birthday party, volunteer Sarahi made her annual spring-fling cake—my absolute favorite.

I posted a photo of myself exclaiming over it on Casa's Facebook page: "I give thanks to my family, friends, and a lot of complete strangers who have been a source of strength, courage, and inspiration. And, of course, I give a big thank you to the Creator, who chose the Casa community to show love and hospitality to the 1,248 guests who have stayed with us. All the time that we've dedicated to this home is totally worth it when we see families being put back together!"

One by one, our guests that night were chauffeured to the airport or bus station. Debbie emailed me from the airport about the Guatemalan man she accompanied. When they arrived at the gate, they met a friendly Salvadoran woman who was happy to help him on the other end. The guy kept glancing back at Debbie and waving, as if he couldn't believe what had just happened for him. I pictured Debbie's contented smile as she wrote me, "There is hope in the world. So many people want to show compassion and help."

My brand-new board of directors called Casa de Paz "our happy place." I had drafted some of my closest peers—all energy and enthusiasm, ages twenty-one to thirty-seven, some documented, some not. Andrea and Josh brought experience from the earliest days and their priceless perspective. So did Daniel Ponce de Leon, who never ceased to challenge me while his own theology evolved. Casa was now officially a 501(c)(3) nonprofit. And we had a large enough volunteer pool that anytime a need arose—accompanying someone to court, acting as a bond obligor, depositing family-sent money into a detention account, translating for someone at an ICE appointment, sponsoring a person to help them gain bond release—a volunteer always responded within five minutes. *Five minutes!* That was the luxury of an email list of more than five hundred names gathered from our volunteer trainings. I didn't appreciate that kind of scale until a friend joked, "Ask a pastor how easy it is to get five people to volunteer for *anything.*" My friend Wayne Laws, a social-justice pastor I speak with at immigration events, relishes the sheer variety of Casa's opportunities to serve. "Because of that, the work has a ripple effect throughout the community," he says.

Strength of community came fully into focus the morning I got a frantic call from a mountain resort town. A woman about my age, Hannah, left a panicked voicemail that her fiance was being transported to Aurora ICE that day. "His court hearing is on Monday morning," she said. "I would like to visit him in ICE on Saturday if possible." There was a pause. "Honestly, I don't do very well by myself. I need to be around people. Would it be okay if I came there for the weekend?"

I texted back: "You have a place to stay here, all meals provided. Come as soon as you can. You don't have to worry about anything."

I promptly emailed the Casa community announcing an impromptu potluck that night to support someone in need. Several hours later, a dozen people spread homemade dishes across our long table like a homecoming meal. When Hannah arrived, she was astonished.

She and her fiance worked as servers in the same restaurant in the resort town. For seventeen years he had sent his earnings to his family in Mexico. Now, overnight, he and Hannah were frightened for their future.

"We had a couples' spat, raised our voices," she said. But a neighbor with a grudge called the police. No one pressed charges, yet Hannah's undocumented fiance was taken to the county jail.

"He was allowed one five-minute phone call," Hannah said, shaking as she revisited the fear of that night.

She spent $5,000 on an immigration lawyer, having to borrow most of it from her family. As restaurant workers, she and her fiance had limited incomes.

Lorena, a professor at the University of Denver, was especially moved. She tenderly took Hannah's hand, asking, "Do you have someone to go to court with you on Monday?" Jennifer, a doctoral candidate at the University of Colorado in Boulder, volunteered. Someone else stepped up to take Hannah to ICE on Saturday to visit her fiance.

Hannah scanned the faces around the table—a professor, a bus driver, a pastor, a student. She teared up again. "I was told you are a supportive community."

The next day, when Colorado Public Radio rang our doorbell to interview me, I introduced the reporter, Andrea Dukakis, to Hannah and explained why she was here. "Well, Hannah," said Andrea, "would you like to tell us your story?"

Hannah was amazing—so articulate. She laid out how hard it was for couples in their situation and how much the smallest bit of support meant. "How does someone open their home *to a stranger*," she wondered to Andrea, "not knowing them at all?"

To a stranger. Hannah probably wasn't conscious she was echoing the Bible.

Hannah got some relief the next afternoon when she saw her fiance at Aurora ICE. That night, as she lay in bed in the women's room, she read letters left by Casa's guests, and she sobbed. She described the experience to me the next day over breakfast. "Reading one letter after another, I felt God so strong," she said. "So many people came to dinner to support me last night, people who don't know me—scholars, ministers, people of all kinds. This is something." She paused. "It made me wonder, what have I been doing with my life the last ten years besides making money to live?"

On Monday morning, Hannah's fiance was released on bond. On their drive home, Hannah left me a message saying she'd been using alcohol to numb her panic. Since her visit to Casa de Paz, she had no desire to drink at all. A black hole of despair was filled by love—the love of strangers.

I was never surprised by experiences like Hannah's at the Casa. Then something happened that genuinely surprised me. A visitor appeared at our door I never thought I'd see: William Perceval, the new assistant warden at Aurora ICE.

A guest at the Casa freaked a little when he saw Mr. Perceval walk in. But the assistant warden was all smiles. "Hey, I didn't know you were out! Congratulations," he said, offering a fist bump.

Mr. Perceval had a good reputation among those in detention. He had succeeded a couple of assistants after the first one left—years that were not good, according to our guests. That amazing assistant had finally left his job, quitting after the birth of his first child. He couldn't bear bringing home all the negativity of the ICE environment. During the presidential campaign of 2016, he witnessed a huge ramp-up inside the facility. GEO, the private-prison corporation, did a full remodel, as if they anticipated needing more beds. When he left, though, he was proud he'd made Casa known inside. It made a difference to everyone, both immigrants and guards, knowing there was a place of comfort and security awaiting people when they were released.

Now William Perceval wanted to know more for himself. "I wanted to see where we're sending people," he said in a warm tone. I gave him a tour of the home I was so proud of: basement bedrooms furnished with dressers full of clothes; bunks with nice coverings you'd see in a bed-and-breakfast; a wall mural painted by the artist Jeremy Collins, his image of mustard leaves weaving through the word "Bienvenidos" ("Welcome"); and my favorite area, the downstairs display where guests leave gifts they made from simple materials inside Aurora ICE: keychains formed from gum wrappers, hats woven from yarn, bracelets produced from scraps of all kinds. These were their thank-yous. They couldn't possibly know we were far more thankful for them, real-life heroes who awed us with courage and resilience.

Mr. Perceval noticed the framed cover of *Westword,* Denver's alternative newsmagazine, featuring me in volleyball gear superimposed in front of a prison fence. That cover story, by local journalist Chris Walker, drew a lot of volunteers to Casa when it appeared in July 2016. By then, the Denver Public Library included our brochures in its programs for immigrants; now they requested a written history of Casa de Paz for their Western History archives. I started getting requests from people in other states wanting to start their own version of Casa de Paz. I had just explored something like that with Deborah Cruz, a leader of Advocates for Immigrants in Detention Northwest. She flew in from Oregon for a deep dive together into how to recruit, train, and care for volunteers. That got me thinking about starting regular Casa de Paz immersion experiences. Maybe we could host churches or small groups for onsite training. Anything to help more of our friends in detention.

We received small grants from groups of all kinds, and now we were considered for one from the Church of Jesus Christ of Latter-day Saints. We were recommended to them by the US's very first resettlement agency, Lutheran Immigration and Refugee Services. Basel Mousslly, a new leader at LIRS, had been impressed with our grant application to the agency. With a humble gravitas and a penetrating smile, Basel is LIRS's program manager for detention visitation. We were honored just to be considered by a guy like him. In his home country of Syria, Basel drove an ambulance for the Red Crescent, the equivalent of the Red Cross. He trained some of the White Helmets, the famous rescue workers who brave battlefronts to evacuate wounded civilians. His life was on the line many times, and he did it all as a volunteer. When his fellow volunteers started being jailed and killed, Basel's parents made him promise to emigrate. Now in DC, reviewing applications like ours, he was impressed by Casa's entrepreneurship—*funded by a volleyball league?!*—and that we operated wholly on volunteer energy. Basel mused, "This is exactly what we're looking for," a group that supports itself through the resources around them (read: awesome volunteers! passionate volleyball players!) and that covers as many bases of a detained immigrant's care as possible. We got the grant.

Basel may have been the source of our later recommendation to the United Nations. Globally, people were migrating in unprecedented numbers, and the UN sought model programs offering support to immigrants released from detention. Evidently—and sadly—programs like the Casa's are rare, beyond the diligent faithful who've always advocated for immigrants, groups like the AFSC and Jen Piper. And that's exactly why a UN representative showed up at Casa de Paz that spring of 2018 to study what we do.

As Mr. Perceval took it all in, he kept nodding, smiling, gazing around our house. Originally from the Caribbean, he knew a side of immigration that most citizens—including ICE employees—don't. "I want all the information about Casa de Paz that you can give me," he said. "We'll place it in the packets we give to people as they are released." He said he'd tried to convey to every distraught immigrant what Casa offers, but he hadn't really known for himself. He chuckled, "Someone should write a book about this."

The following week, Winston opened our front door and stumbled into a large bag on the step. It was filled with winter clothes. The donor was Mr. Perceval.

I still found it hard to compute that someone like Mr. Perceval could work at Aurora ICE. I'm sure his philosophy was like the earlier assistant warden's: do what you can for those who need it most. But that spring at the Casa, we saw a trend more disturbing than usual. A lot of our guests arrived from ICE with injuries.

A guy from Ecuador showed up with an open wound. ICE's medical staff hadn't done anything to help him. A young guy from Honduras winced as he limped up the stairs to our living room, accompanied by his attorney, Liz. He had severe testicular swelling and could barely walk. He had limped in agony as ICE guards yelled at him, "Hurry up, hurry up!" When he sought medical aid, he was given ibuprofen and told to walk it out.

"They're all being released because the GEO Group doesn't want to pay for their treatment," Liz said.

When I shared this at a quarterly roundtable I attended, I saw knowing nods. The meeting was held in the office of US Congressman Ed Perlmutter, on West Colfax Avenue. His staff leader on immigration, Jeremy Rodriguez, wanted to hear regularly from advocacy groups. During the 2016 campaign, Jeremy was one of the few political representatives who visited Casa de Paz. He followed up, inviting me to his quarterly meetings, and I was overjoyed to pool Casa's info with others'.

Most of the nation wouldn't have noticed one of the dramatic changes that happened overnight with the 2016 presidential election. I mean, literally overnight. The very next day in Denver, News4 reported a barrage of hate incidents, including a message taped to an immigrant family's door: "Watch your back. KKK." In Aurora, 133 languages are spoken in public schools, and the city's Mental Health Center saw double the number of people show up for help, fearing for their lives. In immigrant communities, life suddenly turned upside down.

Their fears proved real as, one by one, the new administration rolled out policies that threatened their status. In the administration's first 100 days, ICE arrests shot up 38 percent. That meant 41,000 more undocumented people were shoved into the detention system. In those brief few weeks, the GEO Group, the private-prison company that runs Aurora ICE, saw its stock price rise 98 percent.

Brittney Compton, our volleyballer and volunteer extraordinaire, saw the effects on young families in her WIC and SNAP programs. Pregnant women and young moms suddenly dropped out. But why? These preventive programs were meant to improve public health and conserve the country's medical resources. Brittney learned the women's lawyers were advising them to opt out. They got wind that the administration was seeking ways to threaten their federal status and deport them.

Whoa—our government was targeting vulnerable moms and kids? That seemed beyond cruel.

So were the administration's threats to end DACA—Deferred Action for Childhood Arrivals. Young people who'd been brought here by their parents—some as babies or toddlers—were given the promise of a future in the US. Now they lived with the threat of that promise being deported. Why them? Ninety percent of DACA qualifiers had jobs; half of them were in school. I knew DACA students, and they were some of the most courageous, giving, sacrificing people I'd ever met. They were also some of the boldest voices for immigrants' rights, but the new policies put fear and uncertainty into many.

A year and a half later, the aggressive policy changes hadn't stopped coming. Each of us sitting at Jeremy Rodriguez's roundtable saw the effects firsthand every day. The stakes for people we walked alongside were heightening as the months passed.

The news that May morning was grim. RMIAN, the awesome legal pro bono nonprofit, got reports that Border Patrol officers in El Paso were telling asylum seekers, "Turn around, go home, we don't want you here."

Jeremy was alarmed. Asylum seekers were doing what they were supposed to do by law: to present themselves at the border where they made their claim. Turning them away violated both US and international law. Like a lot of people in public positions, Jeremy measures his words and emotions carefully. But his expression held more than concern.

Laura Lunn, my savvy friend from RMIAN, then dropped a bombshell. "All of our clients—one hundred percent of them—are afraid to return to their countries," she said. "Yet right now, asylum seekers at the border aren't being processed—they're being *prosecuted*."

Wait, how could an asylum seeker be prosecuted when they come here the prescribed way?

That wasn't Laura's biggest revelation. "Even when they're not prosecuted," she added, "they're being forcibly separated from their kids."

"*Separated?*" Jeremy was incredulous.

RMIAN was representing more and more detained parents whose kids were taken from them at the border. The separations were part of a then-unknown Zero Tolerance Policy. "Those parents have gone for weeks not knowing where their child is," Laura said. "One mother was told her five-year-old was being taken for a bath, and she never saw him again."

A collective gasp went up.

"How do they know where their children are?" Jeremy asked.

"Most don't. There's an ICE hotline, but the info is delayed. Parents are in the custody of the Border Patrol, but the children fall under the care of Health and Human Services. There's no single database for the two. Communication between them hasn't caught up. It probably won't."

We sat in a shocked silence. I glanced at Jeremy. Everybody did. He was working hard at restraint.

"This," he said, pressing two fingers to his lips, "is infuriating."

He urged us to contact all of Colorado's congressional leaders. "Call them, email them, text them," he said, "and it needs to be constant. When they see communities involved on an issue, it gives them an idea of what's needed. And it helps us to do our job," he said, "because it puts pressure on how things move in Congress. If we can't get an issue to the floor to vote on it, we can't do anything."

Jeremy's mental wheels churned.

"Nobody has a sense of what's happening," Jeremy said. "This is the hardest piece of the puzzle—to get the public informed." He looked around the table. "All of you are doing a lot for the community," he said. "It's the people who aren't directly involved who need to know."

***

Casa de Paz is not political. As my boss, Chris Fowler, at Church Community Builder has always maintained, the work Casa does is for people, not politics. I'm so glad the company has always seen that distinction. Their support through everything I'd experienced with the Casa in six years meant everything. That was especially important because in the coming months I would receive other invitations like Jeremy's. For some political leaders, Casa de Paz would become an urgent destination. The Casa is where fourteen desperate parents, separated from their children, came for support. Hosting them was the hardest thing we ever did.

CHAPTER 11

You Talk, We Listen

Jesus came to prepare us for the kingdom of God,
which has not yet come, as we know only too
well. He told us that the kingdom will be among
us when we love God with our whole heart and
soul, and when we love our neighbor as ourselves.
If only we would do this, not just in words but in
deed!

—J. HEINRICH ARNOLD, *Discipleship*

Almost nobody knew that children were being taken from the arms of their moms and dads at the border that spring of 2018. Yet it had been going on quietly for a year. By the time we heard about it in Jeremy's meeting, thousands of families had been separated.

The one thing most people did know about immigrants then was that public feeling was against them. Viciously. Especially among Christians. It happened almost overnight with the 2016 election. Before that, immigrants were seen differently. Not many of us today remember the reform proposals created by Senator Marco Rubio, whose parents were immigrants. Bill O'Reilly from the Fox News Channel congratulated him on a policy he could use to work with President Obama. Fox's Sean Hannity praised it too, saying, "I have evolved."

That all changed during the presidential campaign. The public was told that the face of immigration was no longer Marco Rubio's parents. It was hordes of marauding criminals ready to storm our borders.

That's when Casa de Paz started getting calls from pastors. "I've waited too long to get involved," one said. "This was my wakeup call." Our monthly new-volunteer trainings usually drew from five to fifteen people. On the first Saturday after the election, forty people packed our living room.

Here was the curious thing about people from my faith background: There was a huge breakdown between ministers and their congregations. A Pew Research study found that nine out of ten evangelical pastors were in favor of helping refugees. But half of all the people in their pews didn't want refugees in the US at all. Pastors wanted to come alongside immigrants, but congregants feared them.

Christians didn't realize they were forsaking their own heritage—a powerful one. The US church has been at the very forefront of modern refugee assistance. It began when Lutherans stepped up during World War II to take in Polish people fleeing the invading Nazis. That was the origin of LIRS. Since then, thirty-seven countries joined together to take in refugees in crisis internationally. Our government relies on nine agencies to resettle the refugees arriving here, all but one of those agencies rooted in a faith tradition. They're our country's officially recognized Samaritans doing the work that Jesus taught, tending the wounds of the stranger left lying by the roadside.

Yet refugees were one of the new administration's first targets. A month after the inauguration, all resettling of refugees was suspended for four months. That might sound like only a bureaucratic delay, but practically it cut a third of the refugees allowed into the country that year. That amounted to nearly 40,000 people. Plus, all Syrian refugees—people fleeing war— were denied entry *indefinitely*. A few years earlier, that would have meant a death sentence for a hero like Basel Mousslly. What about his brave friends back home who were being detained and executed?

I was glad when evangelical leaders stood up with a collective shout of protest. Tim Keller, Max Lucado, Ann Voskamp, and five hundred others signed a letter to the new US president in a massive appeal organized by World Relief. Their letter stated, "We have a historic call expressed over 2,000 years to serve the suffering. We cannot abandon this call now. . . . As Christian pastors and leaders, we are deeply concerned by the recently announced moratorium on refugee resettlement. . . . Compassion and security can coexist, as they have for decades. For the persecuted and suffering, every day matters."

Today, three years later, the United States is nearly dead last among those thirty-seven countries at resettling refugees. In that period, the new administration reduced the number of people we resettle from 110,000 annually to just over 10,000. And it wasn't about cost. Refugees pay back every dime spent to get them to the US, which can be thousands of dollars for families. Repayment starts within six months of their arrival and is complete within forty-two months. After that, every day of a refugee's life contributes to the US economy. To prevent them from coming here leaves trillions of dollars on the table.

So if this new attitude about refugees wasn't about cost, what was it about?

Around that time, I met a new friend at Casa de Paz. Rich McLean is a dedicated lay leader in Catholic circles in Aurora. He connects various groups on immigration, interacting with police, day laborers, public health officials, and ICE's regional community relations officer to make immigrant life work for everyone. Rich works especially to secure health care for immigrants in Aurora, whose hospitals won't accept anyone who's uninsured. "The hospitals will treat children," Rich says, "but if you're an adult with cancer, God help you."

One night at one of our Casa potlucks, Rich heard someone mention the huge gap between evangelical pastors and their congregations. He realized the same gap exists among Catholics—it just looks a little different: undocumented families may make up a large part of a Catholic congregation, but the rest of the church can keep distant from them. "We sit next to Julio in church and ask him who'll win the Super Bowl," Rich said at the table that night, "but we won't ask him about his life. Often, Julio and his wife and his children are living in fear. That's a double shame, because the church may be the only place they feel safe."

Someone asked Rich why more pastors and priests didn't speak out in support of immigrants in their churches. "I think they just don't know what to do," he mused. To change that, Rich organized a conference at Ascension Parish in Denver's Montbello neighborhood. He called it Who Is My Neighbor? after the question put to Jesus. One of the gathering's biggest takeaways was that as Christians, most of us don't *know* our neighbor, even the one sitting next to us in church.

Sister Martha, a nun who opened the conference, described her visits with immigrant families along the Front Range, from New Mexico to Wyoming. The previous week, she said, she visited three families with adolescents who had attempted to die by suicide. The teens could no longer deal with the fear that their parents might be deported. In some immigrant households, young children were left by themselves all day; their parents had to work several jobs because they were paid unfair wages. Those families, Sister Martha said, need a hand to hold theirs. An ear to hear their stories. Arms to offer the simple balm of care.

Rich spoke next, describing an all-church gathering in his own parish called You Talk, We Listen. Church members formed a supportive circle around the undocumented families in their congregation to offer reassurance and support. Tears fell as frightened families described their daily dilemmas over the simplest needs. A short drive to a doctor's appointment was unnerving for them; they could be stopped by police and taken from their families forever.

"So our church started a transportation program," Rich said. "Volunteers drive people to their appointments. We started another program to accompany families to immigration court. We help couples put together a preparedness plan. They need a strategy in place if one of them is detained or deported." All of these practices are so simple—legal, supportive, immensely helpful—and make a world of difference to people we've sat next to in church for years.

Jenny Kraska shared a similar story. She spoke as executive director of the Colorado Catholic Conference, who lobbied on behalf of immigrants at Colorado's statehouse. Jenny handed everyone at the conference a "Know Your Rights" fact sheet from the George W. Bush Institute website. It lists legal talking points for immigrants if they're stopped by ICE or the police.

Jenny told of sitting next to a Latinx mom in church who knew very little English. For years they greeted each other warmly and exchanged small talk as Jenny watched the woman's kids grow from toddlers to kindergartners. One day after mass, the mom asked Jenny for some simple help. She needed to fill out a school form for her kids, but she didn't understand all the English. Jenny was happy to offer a hand, yet suddenly she was overcome with embarrassment. All those years, she thought, she could have been walking alongside this woman more closely—her friend at church!—and helping with simple tasks that probably caused her friend untold anxieties. She'd just never thought to ask.

Deacon David, who helps oversee the Ascension Parish, closed with an admission. It may have been the most profound statement of the day. "I'm ten steps behind," he acknowledged. "Please, tell us what you need. People are afraid to trust their neighbors because they don't want to be turned in. What is needed here today begins with trusting each other."

"This place," Rich added, pointing to the beautiful ceiling of the church, "is a sanctuary. It has to be a sanctuary for us *all*."

A few years ago, my mom was standing over the kitchen sink washing dishes when she connected the term *refugee* to her mother.

Two years before the Nazis invaded Poland, my family, the Kruks, fled their homeland for France. My Polish grandma—Mom's mom—was two years old.

Grandma's father stayed behind to fight the Nazis. Her mother took the kids to central France, where she worked on a farm. For five years, my grandma—from ages two to seven—didn't see her father. They knew he'd been captured and sent to a concentration camp. Then a knock came in middle of night. Grandma's mother screamed, "It's him!"

Shh! he warned. He hugged and kissed them all quietly. But he couldn't stay with them in the house. He had to hide in the forest.

Every day, my grandma watched as her mother took food to the forest and hid it in a hole. Grandma's father came out at night to eat what she'd brought.

The Nazis came, as he'd predicted. They marched my

grandma, seven years old, and her mother to a stone wall and held them at gunpoint for four hours. Soldiers searched the house and scoured the forest. They forgot to look under the bed. And that's where he had hidden.

We've always thought of that as miraculous. Yet my grandmother never got over the sound of thunder. To her, it was the sound of bombs. Whenever a storm came, her legs and hands went numb. It was severe post-traumatic stress, and she suffered it her whole life.

That was being a refugee.

A few years ago, my dad took a job testing computer chips for BMW and my parents moved to Munich. When Anna and I visited them, we all made a trip to that farmhouse wall in France. I saw the spot where my family almost ended.

The Poles, my ethnic ancestors, were the first people helped by Lutherans in the Nazi invasion. What if those Christians hadn't stepped forward? What if they hadn't raised their voices for the stranger?

Mom and Dad saw a poignant kind of reversal of Germany's history in 2015. They were in Munich for the historic first arrivals of refugees, asylum seekers, and undocumented poor from ravaged regions of Asia, Africa, and the Middle East. Germany welcomed one million of them. Dad remembers seeing grandparents carrying their parentless grandkids. My US-citizen parents—descended from Russian Jews and Polish Catholics—remembered, "Do not mistreat or oppress a foreigner, for you were foreigners in Egypt" (Exod. 22:21).

It's crazy to think that our Christian family, along with so many others, could ever forget our own immigrant story beneath anti-immigrant media talk. My friend Caleb Lazaro says it best: "All of us are immigrants, but some of us have forgotten our stories."

Greg Mortimer grieved that so few of his community—evangelical Christians—considered the people demonized by cruel policies. When Greg speaks on behalf of Casa de Paz at public events, I love how he describes the kinship he's found with people in detention, a sort of completion to his faith that he'd missed all his life.

When Greg and Karen married after teaching in China, they wanted their kids to know God through people from various cultures. So they set up house in Five Points, the historic African-American neighborhood near downtown Denver. Greg has a long commute to his job in the northern suburbs, where he's on a technology leadership team presiding over IT services for fifty schools, 5,000 staff, and 39,000 students. But the place Greg and Karen most want to have an influence is on their home block on Lafayette Street. After a gang shooting in the park next to their house, they extended a hand to a grieving neighbor, a gang member himself. The gesture started a friendship that resulted in a memorial barbecue in the park, an annual event that eventually helped move a community from a cloud of anguish to collective joy. Working with their new friend, the Mortimers helped start a community garden that provides fresh produce for the neighborhood and after-school gardening jobs for teenagers.

The Mortimers turned to their neighborhood for a church too. They landed at a multiracial evangelical congregation where my friend Daniel Ponce de Leon attended. When I spoke there one Sunday, something about Casa's story struck a collective chord in the Mortimers' small group. For Antoinette Johnson, who had just joined the group, Casa's story connected to her own.

Antoinette grew up with eight siblings in Indianapolis, raised by a determined single mom. Gunshots weren't unusual

YOU TALK, WE LISTEN   171

in their neighborhood, but one night, things got dangerously chaotic: The Johnsons' house suddenly rattled from stray gunfire. A frightening gang battle had exploded on the street. Antoinette's mom hunched over her kids on the living room floor. When police arrived, they counted seventeen bullet holes in the walls of the Johnsons' home. Peyton Manning, who played for the Colts at the time, came to offer neighbors comfort and encouragement, and he hung out with Antoinette's family.

Greg first heard that story from Antoinette as they drove to Aurora ICE. It was Christmas Eve. Their first visit to detention was going to be bittersweet for Antoinette. Several of her family members had spent time in prison, and she took a lot of trips to visit them. She knew that entering a prison again would be hard, but she wasn't fully aware of the old ghosts that ICE's institutional walls would resurrect.

Greg was astonished, though, that nothing in the stifling environment at Aurora ICE intimidated Antoinette. He was awed by how easily she bonded with the guards. Her presence seemed to magically open doors to people's hearts. There's a shy side to Antoinette's personality—she's an observant, attentive listener—yet when she walks into a room, her spirit fills it.

The immigrants Antoinette and Greg saw that night were two men from Cameroon. Greg's visit with Cedric was electric—alternately sad and enlivening, depressing and uplifting. But hope slowly filled the room like a spiritual presence, and the connection between the two men pierced the plexiglass. Greg was awed.

During that hour, Greg and Antoinette each sensed an energy surging within them. As they left, they were rapt—and hooked. "I absolutely want to keep visiting," Antoinette offered, despite the tension she felt inside. "I don't think I can come every week," she explained, "but walking into that prison brings healing to me. It's something I can't describe."

Antoinette's insights about it were invaluable. "Regular prison is a lot better than this," she pointed out. "You get to hug on your family. You get to bring things to them. You can get them a public defender." She was also struck by how similar her siblings' stories were to the immigrants': "They're both trying to figure out how to live in America."

Greg was convinced the rest of their small group would feel the same. They shared a similar heartbeat: Henry, who connects with people so naturally; Rachel, a widowed mom of two sons; Shant'a, a social worker—all faithful to connect to the world God put before them. He was right. One by one, anybody who was able started doing visitation at Aurora ICE on Sunday afternoons after church. Christina Progress, a gentle encourager from another small group, asked Greg if she could join. She was so struck by her first visit that she recruited four others from her own small group. Within a couple of months, a dozen people from the church were going, and their enthusiasm grew.

All the guards at ICE knew when Antoinette was in the building. Part of her mission was to love them too—that's just her faith. But the best part for her was seeing her new friends in detention smile. "You know you can't fix their situation," she said, "but you can lift them."

"It has been fascinating to watch how interest in visitations has grown organically," Greg emailed me. "I'm an increasingly strong believer that if we can get folks to do at least one visitation, the odds are very high that they will be 'hooked' on the work."

A revolution was starting. Hospitality was invading ICE en masse.

While the Casa community expanded outward, my own family kept gravitating homeward. On the Saturday before Christmas

2017, as friends prepped for holiday parties, Anna and I drove to Colorado Springs. We went to celebrate the two-month sobriety of our brother, David. I love the photo from that day—two sisters flanking their brother, all three smiles a perfect Jackson match.

My brother had more guts than I did. The medication prescribed to wean him off toxic alcohol levels was more than powerful. When staffers didn't give him the right dose, David had a grand mal seizure. He could have died. But he endured, and he gutted out his time there. Later that spring, after his painful breakup with his fiancee, I invited him to move into the Casa.

David settled into the women's room because it wasn't occupied most nights. When it was, he bunked with the guys. For several weeks, David was a fly on the wall, absorbing the struggles, dilemmas, and joys of immigrants. He was moved as he saw the men share everything in common, regardless of what culture they came from. They weren't attached to possessions; they freely gave to each other what they had, even if it was all they had. David was suspicious of one guest—he thought the guy might be a threat to me—but he realized his perception was a cultural difference. At night, he heard their stories, some comparing notes from detention but mostly talking about their families and their dreams. Even if they didn't speak English, David came to identify the warm tones of peace. It gave him a taste of his own. I think he absorbed what our guest Hannah did—that pure human love drives away the deepest gnawing ache.

"Winston blows me away," David told me. Every night, my brother watched Casa's lead volunteer come home from his physically demanding job and host guests. He was always willing to prepare a meal for everyone in the house. Nobody worked harder. And he saved every penny so that if his wife, Izzy, and son, Jacob, could reunite with him in the US, he would have some savings in the bank. That week, I'd seen a video of an immigrant in France rescuing a toddler from an apartment ledge.

I watched it over and over and over. It's beautiful. It's heroic. It saved a life. One of the first thoughts that popped into my head as I watched was, *Winston would do the same thing.*

"His lawyer is bringing his little boy here next month," I told my brother. He would stay in Winston's room. "It'll be different having a kid in the house."

"You'll do fine," David said. "You've got a well-oiled machine here."

David was actually the very first guest at Casa de Paz, back at the one-bedroom apartment. He stayed with me the night he and Dad moved me in. Six years had made a world of difference.

"So, you don't go to church," David said with a grin. "You just *speak* at churches!"

David always had faith. We had just taken two different routes with ours. He had spent the last dozen years in a half-dozen cities, shuttling between California and Texas. And yet our two paths, equally crazy, finally led us to the same address. I think our parents might have been pleased.

"So," I couldn't help asking, "were you surprised I would do this?"

"I'm surprised *anybody* would do this."

It did kind of make sense for the sister he knew. The strong-willed one who wanted to be Florence Nightingale and refused all handholding.

"It's a little bit rebellious, in a way," he said. "You've always been kind of a rebel."

"*Me?*" You never really know what your siblings think of you.

"You always pushed the boundaries with Mom and Dad."

"Any kid does that."

He grinned. "I kinda like it."

We talked about Mom and Dad—their faith, their evangelical conversions, the way they raised us. One, a graduate in psychology from UT-Austin, who gave up a promising career to homeschool us. The other, a tech wizard who commuted long hours to work to give us a life they thought best for us.

David's crystal-clear eyes gradually filled with the image of ten acres of central Texas countryside. A fort built from tree limbs, a BB gun, chicken coops, homegrown food. For me, baking to feed people and a mounting stack of Florence Nightingale biographies. Our parents only wanted the right thing for us and pushed themselves to find it.

"All those denominations," David said. "They were always searching, looking for the truth. They were flexible about that."

"Except in the main things." Loving God. Loving people.

"Except in the main things. Yeah."

CHAPTER 12

Welcome to the Real USA

*Jesus gave us a new norm of greatness. If you
want to be important, wonderful. If you want to
be recognized, wonderful. If you want to be great,
wonderful. But recognize that he who is greatest
among you shall be your servant. That's your new
definition of greatness. And . . . the thing that I
like about it, by giving that definition of greatness,
it means that everybody can be great.*

—Martin Luther King Jr., "Drum Major Instinct"

As Greg's growing group visited people in detention that summer, they were shadowed by a new group of volunteers: college students with InterVarsity, the campus faith group—our very first interns. A half dozen of them from all over the region. Their first visitation was with Perkins, a Christian about their age from Cameroon. Perkins had fled his strife-ridden homeland, and his life was in the hands of an immigration judge. "Perkins is a committed Christian, and he prays for our group every day," Greg told the interns. "He says that by visiting those in prison, as Jesus commands, we're showing what the gospel looks like, and that if he gets out, he wants to join us in the work."

For Ruth, a Colorado College student raised by immigrant parents in Aurora, Perkins' story hit close to home. "Perkins is twenty-one," she said, "and so is my brother. When I visited him, I thought of my brother—'What can I do to help?' My Western approach to life began to change. It had been, first take care of yourself and then your neighbor. But Jesus focuses on the 'we'— our well-being is tied to our neighbor's. I'm only now learning this prison has been darkening my hometown my whole life."

"When you visit, you see the hope draining from people," said Ann, a student at the University of New Mexico. "And you understand why. All these extreme precautions are taken against people who are just looking to be safe. Their only crime is wanting a dignified life. When I tell them about Casa de Paz—the community that's behind them and for them—I see their hope come back."

"InterVarsity's stance is that justice and reconciliation are part of the gospel," says John Grant, an InterVarsity staffer at the University of New Mexico. Yet a lot of Christian students have been conditioned to resist social justice. They think it departs from the gospel. "Our task is how to meet them where they are and help them take steps," John says. "And to remind ourselves that once we were where they are."

Racial hate incidents happen on their campuses—swastikas scrawled on sidewalks, a hijab ripped from a student's head, people being told to go back where they came from. It's especially important to have safe spaces for students of color to tell their personal stories. "They don't have many spaces for those discussions," says Gwen, another InterVarsity staffer at Denver's multicollege Auraria Campus. InterVarsity staffers work to provide them.

One of the interns' first challenges was an emotional one. It came in the form of a buzzing four-year-old. Dark-haired Little Mia zipped up the stairs to our living room, followed by a weary lawyer.

"What a ball of energy," my brother, David, laughed as she raced past.

Little Mia breathlessly stopped at our sofa to deposit her pillow and child's backpack. Her energy brightened the room, and I couldn't help smiling. Within seconds, my heart broke.

"Her mother's deportation will happen this afternoon," the lawyer whispered.

It was a beautiful spring day, and an intern took Little Mia outside to romp.

She had flown in from Iowa, where she lived with relatives. Her mom was in Aurora ICE, having sought asylum from danger in her homeland Honduras. She had just lost her case. Facing that reality, she wanted her daughter with her. She couldn't bear the thought of leaving her child behind for good.

We all knew what that meant. Life was so dangerous in Honduras that people were leaving as if it were a war zone. And they weren't fleeing only to the United States, as most people think. Over the past decade, Central Americans seeking asylum in Europe increased by 4,000 percent. That's how bad it was.

Our wait that afternoon was excruciating. Everybody dreaded taking this precious child to the detention center, where she would be loaded with her shackled mother into a van and taken with other prisoners to an ICE airplane.

"Sarah!" chirped a little voice behind me. "These are for you."

Little Mia handed me a bouquet of daffodils plucked from our blooming back yard.

She had entered our house so happy. David and I will never forget that. It tore me up to see her go.

Little Mia never left my thoughts in the coming weeks. I prayed she was okay. I knew she probably wasn't.

"Welcome to the real USA, outside those walls!"

That was Greg Mortimer's greeting to the guests he picked up at Aurora ICE. His mantra rejuvenated our volunteers as much as our guests (those who understood English). Greg's group was now picking up people released from detention to bring them to the Casa and help them get to their loved ones. The guests' joy can be infectious, as Greg wrote:

> Abdou was so thrilled about being released. All kinds of people had contacted him on Facebook to congratulate him. As we drove to the airport, he had a continuous smile on his face. He mentioned how wonderful it was to see the sky, the lights, the countryside. That night, I was tired from a long week and secretly wishing that I didn't have to volunteer, but the evening turned out to be the high point of the week. Casa is such an easy way to touch on one aspect of the immigrant environment. You go for just one hour to visitation at the detention center and your life is changed. You sit with someone for one hour at the bus station and your life is changed.

The group's volunteers kept increasing. "For the third Sunday in a row, I had to turn away volunteers because we had more than enough to meet our immigrant friends in both shifts," he wrote.

One of Greg's innovations revolutionized my own work with Casa. He discovered WhatsApp, the digital program for live group interaction. Overnight, dozens of Casa volunteers pooled their knowledge to assist our detained friends. Instead of me having to field dozens of texts—about money dropoffs, shifting visitation policies, and courtroom quirks—Greg's group had answers for each other in seconds. The group was so diversely experienced in such a short time, their WhatsApp thread was a virtual classroom on immigrant detention. Anyone could read it and within half an hour have a doctorate in what I'd spent years learning. It was thrilling to see. And Greg marveled over the urgent help it provided our friends who were suffering in detention:

Rhemi is a University of Denver grad student who recently started visiting with us. She asked a question about our friend, Sebastian, in detention, whose fingers were recently amputated. She said Sebastian often doesn't get his medicine from the guards and is in pain all the time; his stumps are always cold and sensitive to even slight temperature changes. Rhemi wanted to get Sebastian some gloves but was told by ICE that those would be considered contraband because they don't serve a medical purpose. So she asked for help on WhatsApp, and within minutes Zaza—an immigrant from Venezuela, and an amputee herself who's in a wheelchair—offered quality advice about bandages. Minutes later, Shannon, a doctor, chimed in. And finally, you, Sarah, weighed in to connect Sebastian with legal help who can advocate for him. All of this in a span of seventeen minutes. Beautiful.

Pooling their contacts, his group found a therapist willing to volunteer to help our friends in detention. They also enlisted fifteen clergy willing to provide pastoral services—bilingual priests, pastors, and a rabbi. But as usual, the responses from ICE were super slow in coming.

Mostly, Greg was impressed and humbled by how powerfully so many non-Christians love "the least of these" as Jesus says. He mentioned the Strausses, a new volunteer couple in his group. They had just decided to sponsor a man in detention who could be released on bond while his case was decided. "They are Buddhists who model a sacrificial life that my Savior requires of me," Greg wrote.

Yet Greg made his own impression on guests. One Friday night, he drove a newly released man, Mr. Chatterjee, to the Sikh temple, a frequent destination for our volunteers. When they arrived, a temple leader took Greg aside and asked him to come back on Sunday afternoon. He was insistent, inviting him to a ceremony and to "bring your people."

Greg showed up with Karen and three volunteers. They walked into a gathering of three hundred people where no one was speaking English. The priest motioned the Casa group to the front, gesturing for them to take a seat beside him.

The service was in Punjabi, so nobody from Greg's group understood what was going on. After a half hour, the priest mentioned Casa de Paz, and they realized they were being talked about. The priest summoned Greg and Karen to take the mic.

"You're showing us such honor," Greg began. "We're Christians, and the Bible says we are to love immigrants and treat them as if they are part of our family," he explained. "After doing this for some time, I have learned one reason why God tells us to do this. It is because these acts bless *us*."

A celebratory meal followed, and Mr. Chatterjee sat next to the Mortimers. "You must know, the ceremony today was the highest honor a non-Sikh can receive," he told the couple. "That is why you were given seats of honor."

"Sir," Greg said, "I only gave you a ride."

Mr. Chatterjee shook his head. "Before you arrived in the lobby at detention, I was scared. I had no idea what I was going to do. This act of kindness meant everything to me. I will feel extreme gratitude for the rest of my life."

Greg shook his head in return. "I was the lucky one," he said, "to be Casa's volunteer that day."

*

"The hardest thing about working with Casa de Paz," Greg notes, "is seeing the sheer evil of for-profit detention." Heartbreaks and anger accumulated for his group, as they once did for me. Greg's group neared a breaking point over a man they visited named Enrique Cepeda, who'd been detained for fifteen months. His wife was raising their two adolescent children alone in Aurora.

The Cepedas had escaped the violence in their home country, El Salvador. Now Enrique was about to be deported there.

He wept for his children when Greg visited him. It broke his heart never to be able to answer when they asked on the phone when he was coming home.

"How old are they?" Greg asked.

"My daughter is fourteen. My son is eleven."

Their ages mirrored the Mortimer kids' exactly. Greg was crushed to think of being separated from Brianna and Gabe for fifteen months—and then possibly forever.

Enrique had made some small gifts for the group members who visited him. Greg realized the gifts were more than thank-yous; they were his goodbye. As for his deportation, Enrique told Greg, "I have God."

Greg found it tough to shake off. "Two simple things are true for me in these visits," he emailed. "I can't seem to get enough of these friends. And I feel heartbroken. I find myself increasingly drawn to these visitations because of the opportunity to weep with those who weep, to try to understand a sliver of the pain they're enduring."

The brutal reality of detention was incomprehensible compared with the reality the group members lived every day. As they watched their new friends suffer, how could they possibly deal with the continual heartbreak? With the anger it led to?

They had at least one strength: each other. They started meeting after every Sunday visit to debrief at a Latinx cafe in a strip mall around the block from Aurora ICE.

Yet Greg identified a second need—a big one. "We don't have a theology of suffering," he said. As a faith group, they weren't prepared to contain the continual anguish of their visits. Any Christian's impulse is to have hopeful answers for their suffering friends. To someone facing deportation—the loss of their family, maybe the loss of their life—they could offer none. On the whole, their evangelical background hadn't prepared them for this. What was the righteous response to the heartbreak, frustration, helplessness, and anger?

I thought of one person who might pastor them through this: Anton Flores-Maisonet. I wished I could have flown the whole group to LaGrange, Georgia, to draw from him what took me so long to absorb through experience. I couldn't make that happen, so I did the next best thing: I flew Anton in. My friend agreed to speak at a Christmas banquet for Casa de Paz volunteers. Afterward, we gathered Greg's group at the Casa to pick Anton's brain.

One by one, the group detailed the deep love they felt for the men and women they visited on Sundays and the grief and frustration they took home from those visits, unable to change their friends' situations.

Anton was impressed by how continually innovative the group was—the tag-team visits, the caring debriefings, the informative WhatsApp threads. "Keep experimenting," he exhorted—that was the apostle speaking. His pastor side instructed, "Keep bearing, keep listening, keep taking care of each other." And the prophet gave them what he gave me: the hard truth about being willing to walk with others in their deepest suffering. Someone thought of Simon, the man mentioned in the gospels who stepped up to carry Jesus' cross when he no longer could. Like the gifted pastor he is, Anton gave us new eyes to see.

Cedric, the very first person Greg visited on Christmas Eve, lived up to his noble name. The broad-shouldered young Cameroonian had a humbling effect on his Casa visitors. His most striking traits were his quiet optimism and the moving way he held his chin upward as he spoke, with respect. It was by chance that I matched Cedric one week with a brand-new volunteer visitor. Kathleen Mullen is a retired lawyer in her seventies with a diminutive frame and a voice so soft that you wondered how juries ever heard her. Yet her kind blue eyes conceal a laser focus. I'm sure Cedric was pleased to have such an attentive listener as he detailed his flight from his government's brutal violence. For Kathleen, the scar curling upward from Cedric's brow corroborated what she heard.

Kathleen's legal instincts told her that Cedric might qualify for asylum. "I don't know immigration law," Kathleen emailed me, "but I would like to hire someone for Cedric."

On the day of Cedric's hearing, four of us from Casa sat in the far back of three rows of benches. Kathleen was allowed to observe from the second row. The only others in the courtroom were the bailiff and the court reporter; the US Department of Justice lawyer, who sat at a table on the right; and the defense lawyer Kathleen had hired, at the table on the left, next to her grateful client, Cedric.

The judge asked our friend his story.

Persecution is too clinical a term for what Cedric's minority group endured at the hands of Cameroon's dominant-culture government. The reality was a horror show. Cedric was a peaceable student, but when he saw minority villages being burned, he was compelled to join his fellow students in protests. The police crackdown was swift.

Cedric was jailed for three days. For two straight days, police beat him with batons. The scar lining his brow was no longer a mystery to us. It broke my heart—and angered me—to think of this gentle man being beaten nearly to death by a government squad.

Every so often, the judge questioned Cedric about a detail. His attorney was quick to supply evidence she had retrieved from

Cedric's family in Cameroon. The judge examined it and then asked Cedric to talk about it. "Yes, my honor," Cedric answered in the formal phrasing he knew.

It was nerve-wracking. All of us knew that within an hour or two, our friend would be either released into our warm living room or sentenced to step off a plane in his striven country, where, according to humanitarian reports, he would be arrested immediately, shackled, shut into a windowless police van, and never seen again.

I panicked whenever Cedric was unsure of a question. Trauma causes a lot of immigrants to confuse events and dates, which is almost always fatal to their credibility in court. And without help, evidence is hard to obtain from a detention pod. I'd seen so many unrepresented people end up deported. Thankfully, Cedrid had a lawyer to help.

Cedric's attorney finally rested her case. It was the Department of Justice lawyer's turn. He had alternately scribbled notes and examined documents as he listened to Cedric's story. Now he asked pointed questions of his own. They were thorough, but he didn't take long. "Your Honor, the government recognizes the defendant as a credible witness," he said. He conceded the case.

The judge smiled and made his final ruling: Cedric won. He was an official asylee in the United States. The judge seemed happy for him. And he commended the DOJ lawyer for his decision to concede.

Kathleen allowed herself a smile. What she had done for our friend Cedric was so generous, and I was so incredibly grateful. The lawyer she'd hired shook our hands, thanking our group. "I've heard so much about Casa de Paz. I'm glad to finally meet you."

"I'm so glad Kathleen was our volunteer," I said.

A retired woman's simple kindness—visiting an immigrant in detention—led to something extraordinary. It saved his life.

The preciousness of life came home to me with the arrival of the greatest gift I was ever given, my niece, Gabriela. The little angel's birth was anything but smooth. In the seventh month of her pregnancy, my sister, Anna, had a baby shower on a Sunday afternoon. On Monday, she had labor pains. Javier rushed home from his library job to take her to the hospital. Neither was prepared for the doctor's orders: "You're having your baby tonight. You need an emergency C-section."

Gabi's umbilical cord was coiled around her neck. Surgery was urgent. Not even her father, Javi, would be allowed in the room for it.

Tiny Gabi was delivered fourteen weeks premature. Her little red body lay vulnerable in an ICU incubator, limbs stretched north and south with tubes running in all directions. I knew the moment I saw her I would die for her.

Anna got to hold her daughter for the first time on Mother's Day, May 14. Gabi has her daddy's dark hair, both parents' gentle nature, and her mommy's quiet force of will. The docs called her feisty. It took a lot for our little angel to survive.

Holding her for the first time, something shifted in me. Anna says she saw it happen. A crazy love filled my heart and took me over. In an instant, Gabi was my north star.

Maybe it was because I spend every day with families who can't be together that I appreciate mine even more. When I learned Anna's C-section might prevent her from birthing again, I assured her and Javi, "I'll be your surrogate."

At Casa de Paz, I rarely had an unscheduled hour on any given day. But when Gabi arrived, I suddenly found large windows of time on Mondays and Wednesdays to coo over my niece. Multitasker that I am, I eventually found a way to combine my two great passions: I filmed Casa videos for YouTube, and guess who starred? Gabi became a regular object lesson on the importance of families.

I could not stop talking about my niece, even with Casa's guests. Mom was there the day I showed pictures of Gabi to a sweet, wounded man from Central America. His face had been burned away almost completely by a drug cartel. Even after reconstructive surgery, his face remained disfigured.

"Her name is Gabriela," I enthused to him.

His eyes lit up. "My name is Gabriel!" he said. He dug into his pants pocket and produced a small, woven ring bearing his four-letter nickname: G-A-B-I.

He had made the ring in detention. "Please," he urged, "give this to Gabriela."

Mom and I knew he had made this for his family. Everyone in detention thinks of their loved ones nonstop, and no doubt he was going to give the ring to a family member the next day when he reunited with them after his long bus ride. But I accepted it from him.

"Thank you," I said. "It's beautiful."

His smile slowly turned sad. He said he dreaded stepping off the bus the next day. He was afraid his parents wouldn't recognize him.

I choked back tears.

"They'll know you," Mom assured him. "Your mother will recognize your eyes. And they'll know you by your heart."

Real people facing real crises comparable to so little in an average US person's life—it was changing Greg's visitation group. His words about it were instructive:

> For well over a year now, I have sat with more immigrants than I can remember who have reflected on their pain when I visited with them. Their conversations with me have mirrored

so many psalms of David: weeping, crying out about how God seems to have forgotten them, then talking about how they serve a God who loves them; and even though their circumstances are horrific, they ultimately come back to reminding themselves that God is with them and for them.

I have repeatedly been blown away by these conversations. I often leave Aurora ICE feeling like I am unworthy of the people whom I visit; I count it an extreme privilege to sit with them while they work out their salvation in front of me. I am increasingly convinced that because of my friends in detention, I have a deeper and more visceral understanding of the heartbeat of God. I originally started visiting immigrants in detention because I thought I was going to "help" them. Over time, I have come to realize that I need them, and the main reason I go nearly every Sunday is because they help me—in profound ways that I do not really understand—to become reoriented in my relationship with my Creator.

Today, the evangelical tradition is a culture that is mostly all about the opposite of suffering. Roughly 40 percent of the psalms are songs of suffering and lament, but only a tiny percentage of evangelical worship songs have anything to do with suffering and lament. I think this is a gaping and problematic hole in our faith tradition.

In Roman times, the cross was universally understood to be an extreme sign of suffering, and nearly everyone had seen people brutalized and killed on crosses. So when Jesus called his early disciples to take up their cross daily and follow him, there was no mistaking what that meant. It was a call to extreme suffering.

Your friend the author Matthew Soerens says that roughly 85 percent of the immigrants who come to this country are Christians when they arrive or become Christians shortly afterward. This seems consistent with the folks we meet at

Aurora ICE, and they share and model for me what it looks like to suffer well, in accordance with the gospel. Non-Christian volunteers often tell me that the immigrants they visit want to talk about God with them. The volunteers don't seem to be troubled by this; they are usually simply telling me that they don't know what to say. So I encourage them that—as long as they are comfortable with it—we are there to talk about whatever our friends in detention want to talk about. It dawned on me that countries like Cameroon, Ghana, Cuba, Venezuela, Nicaragua, El Salvador, Honduras, Guatemala, and Mexico have inadvertently become missionary-sending countries. The missionaries from those countries are self-funded, and they come to my back yard and routinely share the gospel.

We all know that this is a profound journey. Years ago, I heard John Perkins preach on Luke 4:16–21. He said that Jesus preached the gospel to the wealthy on his way to the poor, and that we need the poor and the oppressed and the marginalized in order to understand—to the extent we are able—the kingdom of God. In ways that I could not have imagined, my friends in detention are helping me understand that.

The journey continues. Blessings to you, for letting me join you on it.

Every human emotion is contained in the psalms. For several millennia, those songs have served as the hymnal for the people of God. And Greg was right: there is no emotion that God's people aren't allowed to bring before him.

As the events of that spring mounted, I watched a video of a group of young people slipping in the mud of the Rio Grande. They were from El Salvador. They had crossed the river hoping to find peace after fleeing violence. As I watched their struggle, something rose in me to a level it never had before: white-hot righteous anger.

One of the InterVarsity interns, Lauren, returned to the Casa after a visitation. "I talked with a mom today," she said. "They took her son from her at the border."

We were aghast. "Where is her child now?"

"She doesn't know," Lauren said. "When I asked her, she guessed, 'Maybe Arizona?'"

I called Laura Lunn at RMIAN. I asked if they knew how many of these parents were being detained at ICE.

"By our count so far, it's fifty," she said.

I knew I would have no peace until we got them out.

CHAPTER 13

I Don't Know Where My Daughter Is

What matters now is not a mere professing of faith. Now the crucial thing is whether one is found in the power of faith to the end.

—IGNATIUS, *The Early Christians*

When Rosa entered the door of Casa de Paz, I thought of my very first guest from detention—the tender flower Flor. Both women were Guatemalan, indigenous, and slightly built. Both spoke a rural dialect very different from their rough Latin American Spanish. But the similarities ended there.

Flor had come to the Casa with wonder-filled eyes. She was dazzled by streetlights, four-lane traffic, and swirling snowflakes that stuck to her hair. Now, at the height of Zero Tolerance, Rosa was a different picture. Her eyes were vacant. She barely kept her balance as she ascended the stairs to our living room, her shaking hands unable to grip the railing. Rosa moved as any mother would whose seven-year-old daughter had been taken from her.

The border officers who enforced the "family separation" policy surely didn't know her story. In her home country, Rosa was raped by a man who infected her with a sexually transmitted disease. Later, when she met a man she would marry, he was okay with Rosa's condition. But once they married, he was ridiculed throughout the village. His humiliation grew to the point that he tried to kill her.

Our asylum laws—every country's asylum laws—are meant to protect people exactly like Rosa. Yet those laws had been changed by the new US administration. Those working in the immigration system were now instructed that gang and domestic violence no longer qualified anyone for asylum. Thousands of suffering people were being turned away at the border.

And it had gotten worse. The Zero Tolerance Policy was announced two months earlier, in April. "If you don't want to be separated from your child, don't cross the border with them illegally," announced the US attorney general. "That's not our fault."

In good faith, Rosa had brought her little girl to the border checkpoint in Yuma, Arizona. But when she presented herself to the border officer, he ignored her claim for asylum. Instead, he gestured for her and her daughter to remove their jackets.

"My daughter is sick," Rosa implored in her best Spanish. Her little girl had a lung infection. "You aren't allowed to have these," the officer answered and tossed the coats behind him. Rosa didn't know the icy conditions her little girl would be exposed to in detention. Then, to her shock, another officer appeared and led her frightened daughter away. They would be detained states apart from each other, the mom in Arizona, the daughter in Texas. Rosa wouldn't know where her little girl was for weeks.

From that moment, Rosa couldn't think straight. For two months, she was barely conscious that she was in a prison jumpsuit. She stopped eating. She was not given the medicine for her condition. Every thought was of her daughter.

A pod mate told her that parents were allowed to make one free phone call to locate their child. Immigrant advocates know that's typically impossible, with different government agencies handling adults and children. If you don't have money, you can't afford to make follow-up calls. Rosa somehow finally reached her little girl by phone at a Texas detention center. And when she did, her daughter was crying. She had been struck in the face by another child and had a massive bruise. She was in horrible pain.

Rosa spiraled downward. She was transferred from Arizona to Aurora ICE where she found a pro bono lawyer who took on her case. Rosa's bond release came through funds raised by generous friends of Casa de Paz. People approached us asking how to help separated families. I explained that the minimum bond for immigrants in Aurora ICE was $1,500.

More than a thousand immigrants had come through our door, with traumatic histories beyond compare, yet I'd never seen one in Rosa's condition. Her voice was barely above a whisper. She couldn't speak without crying. After everything this mother had been through—rape, robbery, an attempt on her life—her little girl's removal had been the cruelest act of all.

Our volunteers began hammering the Texas detention center with calls. We wanted Rosa to be allowed to visit her daughter. Each time, we were told no.

Nothing, absolutely nothing, could loosen the grip of fear ruling this mom's mind. I could see her thoughts swirling, "Where is my daughter? How can I get her back? Where is my daughter? How can I get her back?" I took Rosa's hand and slowly, carefully led her downstairs. Maybe it would help to pick out some clothes for her little girl. When she saw a *Frozen* backpack, a crack of relief appeared; Rosa could give it to her daughter when she saw her again. Then we found some bedazzled jeans. The items became tangible hope for Rosa, something she could hang on to, reminding her she would see her daughter again. It was something to keep hope alive.

"The consequences of separation for many children will be life-long." That was the testimony of Commander Jonathan White, director of Health and Human Services overseeing the department that handled children separated from their parents at the border. Once a family was separated, children were viewed no longer as family but as "unaccompanied minors" in the custody of the Office of Refugee Resettlement (ORR).

The ORR's shelters aren't designed for long-term care. Inside them, children aren't allowed to share their food. They aren't allowed to touch one another, so siblings can't hug each other when that may be the only thing to bring them comfort.

The children were traumatized. And there was just one word to describe what was happening to the parents: torture. That was the assessment of Physicians for Human Rights.

That's when Senator Michael Bennet reached out to Casa de Paz. A group of his staff members arrived at the Casa to get our take on what was happening. We detailed the medical neglect, abuse, starvation, and separations.

Our revelations were so devastating that I could tell the staff members had a hard time absorbing them. They listened quietly, at arm's length, as if we might be some radical group. I pointed to a young InterVarsity intern who had a month's experience at the Casa doing visitation and hosting guests. "Lauren, do you want to tell them what you've experienced?" I asked.

She spoke with authority. "You go there and you can't shake it," she said. "The barbed wire, the guards, the metal detectors. You get inside and across from you is this tiny woman distraught over her six-year-old son. She doesn't know where she is, much less where her son is being held. She hasn't been able to speak to him for months, and she doesn't have money to track him down. You see her losing hope. I didn't realize the extreme brokenness."

The senator's staff were rapt. They saw our country's immigration practices through a young person's eyes. "Here, fill this out," whispered Eva, the lead staff member, offering me a form. "We can try to follow the case. Maybe we can expedite it." She offered a reassuring nod. "We'll be in touch."

A week later, Senator Bennet met with us in person. Lauren had made an impact.

On the day Rosa left Casa de Paz to stay with relatives, something big happened nationwide: The administration reversed the Zero Tolerance Policy. Enough pressure had mounted. Families were no longer being separated at the southern border.

But that didn't help the 2,000 children already separated from their parents. Instead, it got worse for them. As parents awaited a decision on their asylum case, they weren't allowed to reunite with their kids. If they wanted to be together, the parents could sign a form to deport themselves. It was outlandish! Many of the parents could win asylum, saving their families from mortal danger. Instead, they were advised to return to that danger if they wanted their children with them in the meantime.

A friend of Rosa's in detention did it. A fellow Guatemalan, she signed a form to be deported and was sent back to her home country. But she wasn't reunited with her child. Now in Guatemala, the mom was frantic, calling ICE every day asking, "When are you sending my child to me?" She was answered with silence.

One by one, as moms in Aurora ICE were released on bond, they were directed to Casa de Paz. And that's when the heaviest work we ever did began.

All who arrived were like Rosa. A few could muster a smile, relieved to be free and welcomed into our volunteers' outstretched arms. But all carried the same hollow core. Their search for their children was desperate.

That week—on June 30, 2018—protest marches were held in all fifty states. In Chicago, where the heat index was 100 degrees, the march down Michigan Avenue stretched a mile long. In New York, the march covered the Brooklyn Bridge. In Washington, DC, 30,000 people gathered at Lafayette Square across from the White House. Banners read, "Families Belong Together," "The March to Reunite Families," "Keep Families Together." It was a collective out-cry for the Rosas of the world, saying, "We see, and we won't sit by."

And then they went home.

"When some people hear 'direct action,' they think of going to the streets to protest," says Lisa Martinez, "yet that's only one of many forms of advocacy." Lisa is one of the University of Denver's deeply reflective professors whom I'd gotten to know. She knows full well the power of visible protest, but she also knows that dedicated followup work is just as important. It's why she sends her students to volunteer at Casa de Paz—cooking meals, visiting people in detention, talking to them over din-ner. "Volunteering at the Casa feels to them like more tangible change because they're interacting with people directly affected by immigration policies. They're complementing the work being done to change the laws."

Casa de Paz provided that complementary work for hun-dreds of Denver protesters who weren't content to just go home. They wanted to do something, and the Casa offered that opportunity. Four days after the nationwide marches, our next volunteer training was scheduled, usually a gathering of five to fifteen people in our living room. Days before the event, 193 people had signed up.

I wasn't going to turn away a single person who wanted to help our friends in detention. So I started calling churches in Denver to see if they had room for us. Meanwhile, the signups kept increasing. The day before the training, three hundred people were scheduled to come.

I was in over my head. Rumblings in my stomach.

"Sarah," my mom said, "I'm praying that a volunteer coordinator will step forward tomorrow."

"Uhhh," I stammered, searching for the most gracious response I could offer, "I don't think that's how it works." I probably sounded calm, but inside, a volcano of anxiety was erupting.

Just before 1:00 p.m. that Saturday, a line of cars snaked north and south along Dahlia street toward the entrance to historic Montview Presbyterian Church. The congregants weren't the usual Sunday-morning amblers. On this hot Saturday afternoon, people strode inside with a brisk urgency, some with kids in tow. They were met by a line of twelve Casa de Paz volunteers on laptops to register their names and email addresses. At a minute past two, I grabbed the mic.

"Well, we usually just go around the room and introduce ourselves," I began. The laughter helped steady my knocking knees.

"I'd like for us to have a moment of silence, in honor of the people we'll be talking about today." Then I asked, "Would anyone like to shout out one word that brought you here today?"

"Action!"

"Solidarity."

"Help."

"Community."

"Hospitality."

The responses were wide-ranging, just like the people. Yet at the center of each response was one overriding concept: neighbor. I recalled the insight of my mentor, Anton: "People will want to join you without fully knowing why."

"My word for being here," I said, "is family."

With that, I told the story of Agustín. A father of three, a good man, sitting alone in a migrant shelter in Mexico, worrying over his three children thousands of miles away, wondering how he would get to them. I was reminded anew of my own loving father and what it would have been like to see him taken from us overnight. "It could be a crack in your windshield, it could be a bad lightbulb over your license plate," I said. "You may have never committed a crime in your entire life, and yet some little thing as tiny as these can change your family's life forever. The United States is the only country in the world where law dictates that a certain number of people in the immigration system—between 31,000 and 37,000—have to be detained every day. This isn't because the people being detained committed a crime. Those numbers include people you may know. People like Agustín. And right now, more than a thousand of them are sitting in a windowless building just a few miles from here."

I spoke of Casa's humble beginnings. "None of this is rocket science," I said. "What do you do when a friend calls and says, 'Hey, I'm in town and I need a place to stay, maybe something to eat, and a ride to the airport'? You don't freak out about it. You don't need training to put them up. It's simply about being a friend."

I spoke for nearly an hour, the three hundred faces before me intent, soaking in every story of our immigrant friends, every hardship and joy experienced alongside them. For anyone who ever attended a humble vigil of three people standing in the dark outside a detention center, or watched protest marches on TV and wondered, "Will anything come of this?" that afternoon at Montview Presbyterian answered them. There was a place, a house of peace, for everyone to love their neighbor as themselves.

That evening, I got an email from someone who'd been there that day. "This may sound somewhat forward," wrote Lillie Shobe, "but could you possibly use help from a volunteer coordinator?"

I turned to my mom. "Read this," I said. "And thank you for not being the sort of mother who says, 'I told you so.'"

Lillie came over that night. A paralegal, she had heard about Casa de Paz through her own client in detention. Lillie had worried for the woman, a Central American whose mental health had spiraled downward at possibly being deported. Then, gradually, the client improved, with a peaceful calm. Lillie learned she was receiving regular visits from Casa volunteers. That's what brought Lillie to the Montview training.

"Immigration lawyers are overloaded with cases. Advocates and social workers are exhausted," Lillie said. "It's so obvious what's needed for people in the immigration system—the human connection. I now have a deeper understanding about the potency of Casa's work. Human love literally saves lives."

Donations poured in from a wide range of sources—friends of the Casa, strangers, fundraisers held by music groups, beer brewers, churches—totaling $45,000. One by one we bonded out thirteen distraught moms and a dad from Aurora ICE. The next week brought the best news of all: A federal judge ordered the US government to "release and unify" the separated families. Parents being released around the country would be transported to Texas, where they would reunite with their children.

A media storm suddenly fell on Casa de Paz. Journalists were directed to us by churches and news stations that told them, "Talk to Casa de Paz. They know what they're doing." I was used to giving interviews, but there were too many to handle, some from international outlets like *The Guardian*. We decided I would make a YouTube video to serve as a press conference. After that, I did an interview with the Canadian Broadcasting Corporation.

"Casa de Paz has been open for six years, and we've hosted

more than one thousand people who've been released from detention centers," I told the anchor, Michael Serapio. "But there is a stark difference between the immigrants who've stayed with us after being released from detention and the guests whose children are still being detained. You see it in the parents' faces immediately. They are absolutely terrified over how their child is being treated, and whether they'll ever be able to see them again."

"The administration has promised to reunite these families as soon as possible," Serapio said. "Does that guarantee mean anything to the people you work with?"

I thought of my niece, Gabi, and I answered the way my sister would. "That promise doesn't mean anything until their child is safely back in their arms."

If Gabi were separated from Anna, I would not let anyone on the job rest for one second until my family was reunited. My whole family would be banging on some agency's doors until it happened. Again, I thought of Agustín, a dad who stopped at nothing to be with his children when no agency would help him.

I knew that no government agency in south Texas was going to help reunited families with post-release the way they needed. No one from the government was going to do what a hospitality community does, welcoming them with a hug, serving them a warm meal, and seeing them to their final destination.

I was going to south Texas representing the Casa community.

The sprawling Basilica of Our Lady of San Juan del Valle, near McAllen, Texas, is like a Catholic Disney World. It takes up several city blocks with a massive visitor center, a huge cathedral, family service buildings, a Catholic Charities office, and old barracks buildings turned into hotel rooms. All the released parents and children who were to be reunited stayed there.

I went there to be a familiar face to the disoriented moms we'd hosted at Casa de Paz. To take them for a meal, buy them snacks or toiletries for their trip, and hold their hands if they needed help getting through the trauma they had just endured. Yet nothing was happening. All the windows of the barracks rooms had the curtains shut. No one was around.

The next day, when no official could tell me anything, I decided to visit a place I consider one of the most important on earth: the migrant respite center near the downtown bus station. Like so many things of great value, its appearance is humble—a low-slung, one-story building that might once have been a community meeting hall. Inside, loving care is extended to hundreds of migrating adults and children every day, through meals, showers, travel kits, clean clothes. On one side of the center's large open room are rows of blue, molded-plastic chairs, where migrant families sit waiting to be helped by a half dozen volunteers manning a row of tables.

Most have just been released from Border Patrol, some with bracelets on their ankles. The volunteers sit with them to find out their needs—food, health, and their ultimate destination in the US. Some migrants appear relieved, glad for a stopover respite amid their long journey. Others look concerned, as if fearful their children might be taken from them. In one corner is a carpeted play area for kids, with a playhouse, activity tables, and floor maps. Puppets and playdough provide outlets for expressive play, a sort of first-line triage for the trauma of their journey. This amazing place—a kind of mega Casa de Paz—was started in 2014 by a huge-hearted nun named Sister Norma Pimentel. Sister Norma was stirred with compassion for the thousands of unaccompanied children who came to the border near McAllen that year desperate for help. Sister Norma approached the Catholic Church for support and opened the center. Since then, it has operated twenty-four hours a day, seven days a week, 365 days a year. The center was so moving to see—a living, pulsing representation of what it means to be a neighbor. I know of other hospitality homes across the country, some run by just one person. Together, all of them form a powerful link to bring the compassion of heaven to earth.

The next day, reunited families at the basilica were released. My first pickup was a mom we had hosted and her happy, chatty thirteen-year-old son. The boy's joy disappeared when we were pulled over on the highway by a Border Patrol vehicle. "Where are their orders?" the officer demanded.

This was exactly why I had come. Jen Piper had warned me of immigrants being "double-detained," incarcerated even after they'd been legally released. It could happen if a single sheet of paper was out of order.

The boy didn't speak much after that encounter. It was so sad, so unnecessary, so maddening.

That afternoon, I was cheered when a hyperactive five-year-old couldn't contain his excitement. "There's the flag of the United States!" he pointed out as we passed a car dealership. "It has fifty stars!"

But when we entered the airport terminal, the little boy grew quiet. He was preoccupied with the security process. "Do we have to go through it?" he asked with a worried look. "What do they do?" Seeing his fear shattered my heart. An anger rose in me over what this vivacious young innocent had been through.

When I picked up a mom and her seven-year-old daughter, the girl didn't speak a word. Her mother explained the child hadn't said anything since they were reunited. A friendly flight attendant tried to pin a pair of silver wings to the girl's sweater, but she recoiled. She didn't want anyone touching her.

I must have felt every emotion under the sun that day. What did the moms feel? Like the psalmist, even with the heaviest heart I kept hope. It helped to see them reunited and boarding planes on their way to welcoming arms somewhere.

Back at the hotel that night, I updated Casa followers with a YouTube video on our progress. A volunteer messaged back: "So after all this time, you're finally getting your pina colada at the border." Haha, if only!

I tried to relax but couldn't. Images of the kids shutting down their hearts haunted me. And there were still other moms and kids to be reunited.

If it were your family, you wouldn't give up. And I saw my family in all of them.

Fifty parents had been sent to the border from Aurora ICE. I helped all of the ones we had hosted at the Casa, as well as others directed to me by Denver lawyers. All told, I was in south Texas for five days. On August 1, my last day there, 9News in Denver skyped me into their broadcast. I reported that all the moms and kids who'd come through Casa de Paz had been reunited and made it to their destinations.

Over the previous month, we had hosted fourteen parents, all crippled by fear for their absent children. Their pain had been so extreme. It brought some relief to know they were all in places of peace now.

I had absorbed a lot of that pain. That night, as I watched *The Bachelor*, I was suddenly overcome by sadness. I started sobbing and wasn't able to stop. I had no one to celebrate with, no significant other to say, "How did it go today? You make me proud."

More than two thousand children in the system were still unmatched to their parents. I cried myself to sleep.

The next day on my drive to the airport, I saw a billboard with a stark, simple message—black-print words against a white background:

Tell the kids I love them.

—GOD

The separation crisis was traumatic for anyone involved at any level. Yet even as its terrors became public, in nearly every church where I spoke, people focused not on the devastated families I'd met but whether immigrants were breaking the law. I repeated over and over, "By far the vast majority are coming here lawfully, the right way." Why didn't it matter that the law wouldn't protect families?

By then, I'd handled hundreds of insulting posts on Casa's Facebook page. That included dozens of hate posts. My sister, Anna, remarked on how calmly I dealt with them. Then, a week after I got back from south Texas, a post appeared that I couldn't treat lightly. It came from a stranger: "We should hunt you down."

There's no chill like the one that follows a death threat.

Casa friends rallied beautifully. A group volunteered to install security cameras, others to patrol the house. You never expect a death threat to come from doing simple church work. Especially the commandment to love your neighbor.

I was coming face to face with a truth that every young Christian is taught but that we take less seriously as adults: Following Jesus has a price. For many around the world, it includes the ultimate price. I'm always aware that any threat I may receive doesn't compare to the price paid every day by migrants around the world—from the threat that sends them fleeing, to the dangers of their journey, to the traumas and hardships and threats that many face once they arrive. Their courage inspires me.

On Friday night, I felt very loved when Casa volunteers threw a surprise birthday party for me. The icing on the cake was celebrating it with a young woman who had just been released from detention and whose birthday was the day after mine. The next week I sent out this update:

"Last week was a busy one at Casa de Paz: (1) We hosted twenty-two guests—the most ever in one week! From El Salvador, Eritrea, Mexico, Russia and Fiji. (2) I received my first death threat . . . Who knows what next week will look like. It's always an adventure around here."

Summer was ending and the InterVarsity interns looked forward to new school sessions. What a summer for them. They had run a race and, in my mind, they had won—connecting to international neighbors in detention, serving and supporting those we hosted, leaving such a powerful imprint on a US senator's staff that it drew the senator himself to know more.

"My friends will think this internship was a big waste of time and money," said Faith, a student at the University of New Mexico. "They'll say I could have been building up my resume. But halfway through, I thought about the woman in the Bible with the alabaster jar." She was talking about the gospel scene where a tearful woman anoints Jesus' feet with an expensive perfume. Religious leaders criticized the woman for her impracticality, saying the perfume could have been sold and the money given to the poor. But Jesus honored her, saying her story would be told throughout history. No small act of love is wasted or lost, and they all have enormity in God's kingdom. The interns took that truth home with them.

Ann, the other student from UNM, said to me, "You went to the border, and you saw, 'This is a problem.' You had no resources, no education, and you went out and built this," she said, gesturing around the room, "this incredible infrastructure—*for them*. It reminds me of Moses. When God called him to lead Israel, he answered, 'Lord, I don't have the ability to do it.' But God said, '*I* will do it.'"

I wiped a tear at that. Some joy you just can't contain.

I make a point to take Sundays off, pulling myself away from the Casa and anything work related. That has to happen. But the next Sunday, I got up, showered, got dressed, and went to church. I wanted to do something I hadn't done with my whole heart for a long time: worship God.

Your Kingdom Come on Earth

> *In Jesus' resurrected presence, the invisible*
> *kingdom of God has become visible reality. The*
> *word has taken shape, love has become real. Jesus*
> *showed what love meant. His word and life proved*
> *that love knows no bounds. Love halts at no*
> *barrier. It can never be silenced, no matter what*
> *circumstances make it seem impossible to practice*
> *it. Nothing is impossible for the faith that springs*
> *from the fire of love.*
>
> —EBERHARD ARNOLD, *Fire and Spirit*

I woke to music. Someone was playing a guitar in the living room. He sang in a low voice. Most mornings are quiet at Casa de Paz. That isn't quite a rule, but almost all of our guests keep it down out of respect for others. The music I heard that morning had joy in it. I could accept joy instead of quiet.

I walked out in my volleyball sweats with my hair up and found a guy sitting on the couch. Oh, yeah, David—pronounced *Daveed*—a Guatemalan youth pastor just out of detention.

"Tu cancion es hermosa, David," I said, complimenting him on his beautiful song. He grinned like an overgrown kid. Crewcut hair, gapped teeth, sunshine beaming from grin-squinted eyes. I could tell he'd written the song himself. It was about life in his pod on the second floor of Aurora ICE. Life was like the stairs he climbed there, the lyrics declared. Each day was "sometimes up, sometimes down." *Just like a youth pastor,* I thought, *constantly seeing lessons in the everyday, conveying them to absorbent young humans.*

I thought of someone who excelled at that very thing. "My mother is coming over today," I told him. "She'll want to play music with you." He would meet the queen of homeschool moms who wrought object lessons from everyday life.

Several months later, my mother joined in another kind of music, with another David—my brother. Our David had colon cancer. My father flew from his job in Germany as David began chemo treatments at Anschutz Medical Campus in Aurora. One night, after enduring eleven hours of poison dripping into his veins, David led our family into a quiet room where patients and visitors could relax. It has a grand piano, and that's just what David needed. He looked like so many other patients there, his hair a-whack from lying against a pillow all day, yet magnetic in demeanor and handsome in the street clothes he insisted on wearing downstairs. His back straight like a concert performer's, David summoned the gorgeous notes of his own composition, teased out in the contemplative style of George Winston. After a long day, the sick one in our family settled us with peace. And hope.

Life doesn't stop for anybody or any family. Like David, once a guest steps out of our caring, celebratory home, they still have a full story ahead of them—one of trials and victories. At the Casa, we've heard three thousand stories so far. I marvel that the world could ever contain all the joy and anguish and courage and faith we've absorbed from our guests. My friends at Casa de Paz have loved people from one-third of the 195 countries of the world. *Philoxenia,* love of the stranger, has given us new eyes to see.

Story after story replayed in my head that day as I drove to the lovely mountain town of Keystone. I was on my way to an annual company retreat with Church Community Builder. For the first time, I wasn't anxious about being "out of the office" with Casa de Paz, and I felt great about that.

During that first year in the apartment, I had thought I would be doing Casa de Paz alone. Then Rebeca and Fernando showed me what could be. Then Winston arrived. Then dozens, then hundreds, then Lillie Shobe to coordinate us all. Nowadays, we have no less than one hundred people showing up for each month's new volunteer training.

We attracted more death threats. I worried about the Casa's future if I were gone. The thought so preoccupied me that I once had a kind of waking dream, like a vision.

I was up in the sky, floating above a town on a winter's night. I sensed I was no longer alive. Looking down, I saw a house emitting a powerful orange-red glow. I floated downward to gaze into a window. As I got nearer, the door opened, and I floated inside.

The place bustled. Dozens of people were cooking, laughing, nodding, toasting, filling the living room. Some sat around a long wooden table sharing a meal with guests. Others answered phones or led a guest or two out of the house to give them a ride somewhere. I realized that though I was long gone, the house was Casa de Paz, and it had a life of its own.

That's what I want to happen, I thought.

I grin over an old email that Anton forwarded to me recently. I had written to him a month after I visited El Refugio, "I don't think I'll file as a nonprofit until I see that there's a big enough need." I can picture him laughing. I know so many others who would laugh too.

Kim Oswalt-Rich, Casa's first landlord—and my first onsite advocate—never expected it to become what it is. Kim now manages 120 rental properties in Arizona. She says, "I hope you'll franchise Casa de Paz so I can manage some!"

Nancy Johnson, one of Casa's superstar volunteers, is friendly with a bailiff in an immigration courtroom. The bailiff says she wants to volunteer at Casa de Paz once she retires. Other friends have told me something even more surprising: two Casa volunteers have taken jobs as guards at Aurora ICE! I'm not sure how I feel about that. But if they have hearts like the assistant warden's, the guy who helped so many people in detention, I'll be more than happy. I hope he's happy too in his life after Aurora ICE, jiggling babies on his knees.

Last year, Fernando and Rebeca returned to Denver for a Mennonite conference. I reminded them that they'd scolded me for not sharing the blessing of Casa's work with others. I proudly let them know that they now had two thousand volunteer children. "Dos mil hijos!" they shouted. Casa volunteers made more than one thousand visits to people in detention in 2019. Our T-shirts are noticed throughout Denver. Volunteers who don't know each other bump into one another at the airport, strangers sharing the joyful privilege of companioning a neighbor on their way to freedom.

History Colorado Center features the Casa in an exhibit called *What's Your Story?* about impact-makers in the state. Another Casa installation appeared at Denver's TedX Talk Conference. David Byrne, former Talking Heads front man, recommends us on his website. And Dia Sokol Savage, an MTV producer, has made a documentary about Casa de Paz titled *Welcome Strangers*. Students at the University of Denver are compiling a cookbook from the recipes and stories they learned from Casa guests. And a professor friend at DU received a grant to start a partner program with the Casa, naming me an Expert in Residence—a homeschooler with only a GED. (Take a bow, Nadine Jackson.) All of this ought to encourage anybody who has doubts about what it takes to walk alongside an immigrant neighbor. Broke with no money? Great, you're qualified. No credentials or training? You're hired! No ability? Perfect—God has the ability. You don't have to carry a protest sign; you can bring a meal or offer a ride. Casa's awesome volunteer Antoinette Johnson says it better than any of us: "Stop making excuses. Visit an immigrant today!"

Last year, the United Nations asked me to be a traveling rep for their Human Rights Commission in the Rocky Mountain region, instructing groups on how to run post-detention-release programs like Casa's. Before I do anything like that, I want Casa de Paz to have its own home, fully paid for, with a resident couple I can pay to run it. Thanks to Volleyball Internacional, that could become a reality soon.

Maybe more meaningful than all these things was my encounter with a young Latinx woman who wanted to attend a new-volunteer training. Olivia had known about Casa de Paz but was afraid to get involved because her family was undocumented. Then she gained Legal Permanent Residency, and the draw of Casa's work renewed her interest in a faith she'd left as a teenager. "I am thankful to know that there is someone like you doing so much for people like me and others," she emailed. "If there were a higher power, I'd follow your footsteps because that is love in its purest form."

Olivia introduced herself to me at the next training. "When I came here and saw the church banner—'Supporting Immigrants and Refugees in Their Journeys of Integration'—I thought, 'Here is what faith is,'" she said. "It's about helping people like my family." Love made the difference. *Philoxenia*. It was winning back those whose idea of God had failed them. Just as it did with me.

As Greg says, the journey continues. And there is work yet to be done. The GEO Group, the private-prison corporation, recently built an annex onto Aurora ICE, adding 450 beds. Despite this, we drew strength from the success of our good friends Freedom for Immigrants, the national visitation network. They made history in California by helping to pass the US's first statewide bills targeting the private-prison industry. They drafted and cosponsored the Dignity Not Detention Act, signed into law by California's governor in 2017 to stop the expansion of detention and create more oversight. That was followed in 2019 by AB-32, outlawing private prisons, both criminal and civil. We were proud to take part in their visitation network, with volunteers providing firsthand stories they could use to shape policies. Now a friend of the Casa, Congresswoman Diana DeGette, is calling for alternatives to detention.

The Christmas after Zero Tolerance ended was the hardest year we ever had at the Casa. So many people suffered in such extremes. And we faced more. Enrique Cepeda, the father of a yet-unborn girl, was about to be deported. He wouldn't see his baby daughter enter the world. His wife was devastated. Thinking about them as I sat in a Christmas Eve service, I couldn't stop crying.

I thought of Agustín, the father I'd met at the border, the man whose story changed everything for me seven years earlier. Because of that simple encounter, I had learned that you can't quit. And that something could be done.

When Enrique's daughter was born, we held a baby shower for his wife. It was like any other shower with silly traditions and frilly outfits for the newborn. We did it because we would want someone to do it for our family. And the Cepedas *are* our family. That's the gospel.

Agustín, wherever you are, we did this in honor of your little girl. We did it for your wife. We did it for your boys, who have missed you. And we did it for you. You are a great dad, one of the very best. And God sees.

As I drive, I picture my mom playing guitar with *Daveed*. The living room resounds with squeaky singing and a lot of laughter.

Two generations, two nationalities, two languages—trading one guitar, playing one song. My inspiring professor friend at UCD, Rene Galindo, puts it best when he introduces me to tell Casa's story to his students: "It's *two* stories, coming together."

I'm saddened to think how many Christians and congregations don't know this joy fulfilled in the Great Commandment. An old friend from Colorado Springs wrote me after a brief joyful stay at the Casa. She paid a visit to a megachurch and said everyone there that day looked miserable.

It doesn't have to be that way. That much is proven by a precious video message from a new Casa volunteer named Chelsea:

> I was feeling extremely hopeless—just absolutely depressed and desperate—praying for God's kingdom to come, to take away suffering and injustice and bring peace to the earth. I never see it happening. I started to believe we have to sit by witnessing human misery until Christ comes back. But today, hanging out with Blanca and Claudia and driving them to the airport was one of the most beautiful experiences. I had the privilege of seeing lovingkindness in people's lives after they've been through so much. I see there is hope in the world, Sarah. Love—real, true love—crosses cultural barriers, including someone's immigration status. Today my eyes were opened that the kingdom of heaven is taking place on earth—and I can be part of it. It was a beautiful reminder that God is writing a bigger story. Thank you, Sarah. Thank you, Casa de Paz.

Anton Flores-Maisonet encouraged me to bring peace. When I did, it brought peace to me. And it's accomplished pretty simply. As Ted Lytle, our great volunteer, likes to remind people, "There are fifteen hundred beds in Aurora ICE. And there are fifteen hundred churches along the Front Range." The math is easy.

My dad is retiring early to be with our family through David's struggle. His dream is to settle near Mueller State Park, in the mountain range west of Colorado Springs. He says a dirt road there opens up to a view of the valley that's stunning. I love his idea. My mother can make a home anywhere—that's been her great gift to all of us. So now I'm picturing my brother and my sister and Javi and Gabi in this place that Dad wants to build.

As I drive along a twisting I-70, winding my way through the mountains to my work retreat in Keystone, I'm thinking of the verse that says, "Now these three remain: faith, hope and love. But the greatest of these is love" (1 Cor. 13:13). My faith had been broken down and built up again by immigrants. Their hope had been restored by the care of strangers, at a place they insisted on calling "Casa de Esperanza." And behind it all is the force of a love that will not let us be estranged. Love—*philoxenia*—keeps winning us back to each other.

I'm thinking too of another mountain drive farther south. I hear in my mind the crunch of a gravel road with a view of Mueller State Park. I'm picturing a certain good meal, something meaningful, like, oh, a couple of slices of pizza. Enjoying a string-cheesy, tomato-saucy dinner and splitting a coke, a bubbly, syrupy, ice-cold one, maybe sharing a straw with someone. A family, together—you can taste heaven.

How You Can Be a Neighbor to an Immigrant

(Because You Already Are One!)

There are dozens of ways, many very simple, to be a good neighbor to someone affected by immigrant detention. Here are beginning resources to help you explore what supportive role you may play. Ask a friend to join you. As the proverb goes, "If you want to go fast, go alone. If you want to go far, go together." Groups in pockets across the country are doing the following:

1. Befriend an immigrant in detention. Lutheran Immigration and Refugee Services offers a pen-pal program and shows how to join or start a visitation ministry (https://www.lirs.org /detention-visitation/). Don't miss their compelling video taking you inside the detention experience, *Locked in a Box: Immigrant Detention*. Also, Freedom for Immigrants' website (https://www .freedomforimmigrants.org/) has a fantastic interactive map showing the more than two hundred detention facilities across the US. (The one nearest you might be a county jail.) It also lists all of the visitation programs in their nationwide network. There may be one near you.

2. Learn what the Bible says about your immigrant neighbors. Ask your pastor or a friend to lead a group Bible study on immigrants and hospitality. Find a book on the church's legacy of welcoming strangers—there are some great ones—and discuss it together. Invite a local immigrant advocate to speak to your group. Consider taking a border trip, as I did; your denomination may offer immersion experiences. Encourage a college student to attend the G92 Conference (G92.org), where Christian scholars and students pool knowledge on ways to be good neighbors to immigrants.

3. Find ways for your church to connect with immigrants in your community. If immigrants attend your church, plan a You Talk, We Listen meeting to surround them with loving support. You can do the same with immigrants in your neighborhood. Organize a transportation program to give undocumented people rides to medical appointments. Accompany them to immigration court or to their check-in meetings. Help vulnerable families develop a preparedness plan in case a parent is detained or deported. If they struggle with English, form a team to help them with everyday tasks like filling out school forms for their children. Approach other churches and civic groups to join your efforts.

The detained immigrant you befriend may have a spouse or partner who's undocumented. If so, offer to take their children to visit the detained parent. Purchase phone cards for the parent in detention to call their family regularly. Ask the facility's program director which detained people never have visitors, then send volunteers to encourage them. Gather a group to make greeting cards to send to people in detention so they don't feel forgotten on holidays. All of these things are simple to do, yet they mean the world to families affected by detention.

Ask lawyers you know to represent an immigrant as part of their firm's pro bono legal work. An immigrant's chances of winning their case increases by 80 percent when they have an attorney. A good resource is American Immigration Lawyers Association (AILA) (www.aila.org). Securing someone's release on bond is a multiple blessing: it allows them to be with their family and to work while their case is in process. It also increases their chance of winning by 80 percent. Sometimes, to secure a bond release, a judge requires an immigrant to have a sponsor to take them in; ask church families or several churches to join together as cosponsors.

4. Urge your congressional representative to end immigrant detention and to call for inexpensive, humane alternatives. For ways to do this, visit freedomforimmigrants.org.

5. For your own growth, try these creative exercises:

Put yourself in the shoes of someone in this book. Turn to any page, find an immigrant, and ask what you would do in their situation. Walk around in their world and imagine their family's realities. Then imagine how that experience would feel if they had the support of an entire church behind them.

Research your own family immigrant history. You have one, unless you're Native American. What were your ancestors' motives in migrating? Compare them with someone's situation in this book. What hopes, motives, and yearnings do your family and theirs share?

Finally, if you want to explore starting a hospitality home like Casa de Paz, contact us at casadepazcolorado.org. We're always here. And we always will be, until immigrant detention ends.

You'll never regret befriending an immigrant. Doing it will change two worlds, theirs and yours. And even your smallest act as a good neighbor ripples outward to the community and into eternity. "Truly I tell you, whatever you did for one of the least of these brothers and sisters of mine, you did for me" (Matt. 25:40).